ISBN 978-1-332-26497-1
PIBN 10306330

1 MONTH OF
FREE
READING

at
www.ForgottenBooks.com

By purchasing this book you are eligible for one month membership to ForgottenBooks.com, giving you unlimited access to our entire collection of over 1,000,000 titles via our web site and mobile apps.

To claim your free month visit:
www.forgottenbooks.com/free306330

HEARING

BEFORE THE

COMMITTEE ON FOREIGN AFFAIRS
HOUSE OF REPRESENTATIVES

ONE HUNDRED THIRD CONGRESS

SECOND SESSION

AUGUST 3, 1994

Printed for the use of the Committee on Foreign Affairs

U.S. GOVERNMENT PRINTING OFFICE

83–526 CC   WASHINGTON : 1994

For sale by the U S. Government Printing Office
Superintendent of Documents, Congressional Sales Office, Washington, DC 20402
ISBN 0-16-046239-8

IMPLEMENTATION OF THE CHEMICAL WEAPONS CONVENTION

Y 4. F 76/1:C 42/5

Implementation of the Chemical Weap...

HEARING

BEFORE THE

COMMITTEE ON FOREIGN AFFAIRS HOUSE OF REPRESENTATIVES

ONE HUNDRED THIRD CONGRESS

SECOND SESSION

AUGUST 3, 1994

Printed for the use of the Committee on Foreign Affairs

U.S. GOVERNMENT PRINTING OFFICE

83–526 CC   WASHINGTON : 1994

For sale by the U.S. Government Printing Office
Superintendent of Documents, Congressional Sales Office, Washington, DC 20402

COMMITTEE ON FOREIGN AFFAIRS

LEE H. HAMILTON, Indiana, *Chairman*

SAM GEJDENSON, Connecticut
TOM LANTOS, California
ROBERT G. TORRICELLI, New Jersey
HOWARD L. BERMAN, California
GARY L. ACKERMAN, New York
HARRY JOHNSTON, Florida
ELIOT L. ENGEL, New York
ENI F.H. FALEOMAVAEGA, American
 Samoa
JAMES L. OBERSTAR, Minnesota
CHARLES E. SCHUMER, New York
MATTHEW G. MARTINEZ, California
ROBERT A. BORSKI, Pennsylvania
DONALD M. PAYNE, New Jersey
ROBERT E. ANDREWS, New Jersey
ROBERT MENENDEZ, New Jersey
SHERROD BROWN, Ohio
CYNTHIA A. McKINNEY, Georgia
MARIA CANTWELL, Washington
ALCEE L. HASTINGS, Florida
ERIC FINGERHUT, Ohio
PETER DEUTSCH, Florida
ALBERT RUSSELL WYNN, Maryland
DON EDWARDS, California
FRANK McCLOSKEY, Indiana
THOMAS C. SAWYER, Ohio
LUIS V. GUTIERREZ, Illinois

BENJAMIN A. GILMAN, New York
WILLIAM F. GOODLING, Pennsylvania
JAMES A. LEACH, Iowa
TOBY ROTH, Wisconsin
OLYMPIA J. SNOWE, Maine
HENRY J. HYDE, Illinois
DOUG BEREUTER, Nebraska
CHRISTOPHER H. SMITH, New Jersey
DAN BURTON, Indiana
JAN MEYERS, Kansas
ELTON GALLEGLY, California
ILEANA ROS-LEHTINEN, Florida
CASS BALLENGER, North Carolina
DANA ROHRABACHER, California
DAVID A. LEVY, New York
DONALD A. MANZULLO, Illinois
LINCOLN DIAZ-BALART, Florida
EDWARD R. ROYCE, California

MICHAEL H. VAN DUSEN, *Chief of Staff*
RICHARD J. GARON, *Minority Chief of Staff*
DAVID BARTON, *Professional Staff Member*

(II)

CONTENTS

WITNESSES

PREPARED STATEMENTS

APPENDIXES

IMPLEMENTATION OF THE CHEMICAL WEAPONS CONVENTION

WEDNESDAY, AUGUST 3, 1994

HOUSE OF REPRESENTATIVES,
COMMITTEE ON FOREIGN AFFAIRS,
Washington, DC.

The committee met, pursuant to call, at 9:50 a.m. in room 2172, Rayburn House Office Building, Hon. Lee H. Hamilton (chairman) presiding.

Chairman HAMILTON. The committee meets today in open session to hear testimony on the Chemical Weapons Convention and the executive branch's request on implementing legislation.

The Chemical Weapons Convention was signed in Paris on January 13, 1993 by 130 countries. It has now been signed by 154 countries. Eight countries have ratified the convention; 65 countries must ratify the convention before it can enter into force, 180 days after the 65th ratification.

The administration submitted the convention to the Senate for ratification last November. Action in the Senate is pending. Following ratification, both the House and Senate will need to approve implementing legislation to establish a national authority in the United States to carry out the obligations and procedures of the convention.

Under the convention, for example, all relevant chemical activities of the U.S. Government or of private industry will need to be reported, declared chemical facilities will be subject to international inspections, and U.S. industry and U.S. citizens may be subject to penalties under such implementing legislation if they violate the obligations of the convention.

On July 28, 1994 I introduced the administration's implementing legislation by request, H.R. 4849. I was joined in introducing that legislation by the ranking minority member of this committee, Mr. Gilman, two subcommittee Chairmen, Mr. Berman and Mr. Lantos, and the Chairman and the ranking minority member of the Energy and Commerce Committee's Subcommittee on Transportation and Hazardous Materials, Mr. Swift and Mr. Oxley. That implementing legislation has now been referred to this committee, the Judiciary Committee, and the Energy and Commerce Committee.

I have asked witnesses this morning to comment on:

The importance of the Chemical Weapons Convention to U.S. nonproliferation objectives; the significance of U.S. ratification and ratification by other countries; verification and enforcement of the convention; and the proposed implementing legislation.

We are pleased to have with us today as witnesses:

The Honorable Martin Lancaster, who has followed the negotiations of the convention in Geneva for several years in his capacity as a House Observer to those arms control talks;

Mr. Donald A. Mahley, who replaces ACDA Director John Holum, who could not be with us since he had to travel to the nuclear test ban negotiations in Geneva. Mr. Mahley is the Acting Assistant Director of Multilateral Affairs at ACDA and head of Delegation for the United States at the Preparatory Commission in The Hague;

Dr. Will Carpenter, who was chairman of the board of Agridyne Technologies and is now vice chairman. Dr. Carpenter retired from Monsanto Company in 1992 as vice president and general manager. Dr. Carpenter has been the Chemical Manufacturers Association representative to U.S. Government negotiations on chemical weapons and now implementation of the convention since 1979; and

Mr. Michael L. Moodie, president, Chemical and Biological Arms Control Institute in Alexandria, Virginia.

The format here will be to proceed by asking Congressman Lancaster to begin with his testimony followed by a question-and-answer period since he will have to leave. Then I will ask the other witnesses to present their testimony as a panel with each presenting a 5-minute summary of the testimony followed by a question-and-answer period for all three.

We are very pleased to have joining us today Representative Glen Browder, who is attending the hearing this morning and has a very strong interest in this Convention and has participated, I believe, in a number of the sessions with respect to the convention. We are honored to have him.

Mr. Gilman, do you have a statement before we proceed to Mr. Lancaster?

OPENING STATEMENT OF CONGRESSMAN GILMAN

Mr. GILMAN. I am pleased to join you in convening this hearing to address ratification and implementation of the Chemical Weapons Convention. While the Senate obviously has constitutional responsibility for ratifying treaties, I believe it is extremely important for this chamber, as well, to consider the important issues raised by that Convention.

Additionally, as we all know, both bodies will have to enact enabling legislation if this treaty is to be finally implemented.

I join you also in welcoming our witnesses today, including Congressman Lancaster who has been a leader and a strong advocate of this treaty for a number of years. I know Congressman Lancaster was in Geneva on many occasions during the negotiation of this treaty, and his continued involvement in securing ratification and enacting implementing legislation is of importance and fully appreciated by this body.

Over 100 years of international efforts to ban chemical weapons culminated in January of 1993 with the signing of the Chemical Weapons Convention. The United States was, of course, one of the original signatories to the convention and indeed was instrumental in securing the accord in this important arms control area. Nonetheless, the CWC raises a variety of issues for congressional consideration. These include issues regarding universality, verification, possible conflicts between inspection procedures and U.S. constitutional protections.

The Congress must also address the question of overall costs of administrative foreign assistance and CW destruction. I am particularly interested in hearing from today's witnesses about Russia's commitment to the treaty, including questions surrounding Russia's continued CW production, failure to disclose full information on its binary program and its record thus far in actual chemical weapons destruction.

Obviously, if this is to be an effective, verifiable and ultimately, successful treaty, it is essential to have the owner of the world's largest stockpile of chemical weapons not only on board but faithfully honoring and abiding by the treaty's tenets. I am not certain that is the case at this time.

We look forward to our witnesses' views on the subject.

Thank you, Mr. Chairman.

Chairman HAMILTON. Congressman Lancaster, we are delighted to have you here. We commend you for your leadership on this issue. We look forward to your testimony.

You may proceed, sir.

STATEMENT OF HON. H. MARTIN LANCASTER, A REPRESENTATIVE IN CONGRESS FROM THE STATE OF NORTH CAROLINA

Mr. LANCASTER. Mr. Chairman, committee members, good morning. I appreciate the opportunity to testify before your committee on the implementation of the Chemical Weapons Convention.

Over the past several years, I have taken a keen interest in chemical weapons and played an active role with the CWC as an observer of the negotiations in the Conference on Disarmament in Geneva. I have continued my involvement by working with the CWC Preparatory Commission in The Hague, which is charged with hammering out the myriad of details which inevitably arise when implementing an agreement of this magnitude.

I have also worked with nongovernmental groups such as the Chemical Manufacturers Association, the Henry L. Stimson Center and the Center for Strategic International Studies in their efforts to broaden both interest and understanding of the CWC through the administration, Congress, industry and the general public.

RUSSIAN RATIFICATION OF CWC

Finally, I have taken an active role in working with representatives of the Russian Government in facilitating the startup of their CW destruction program.

We have heard there is widespread support for ratification of the CWC from both military and civilian communities in Russia. Ratification with absolute majorities will be required within both houses of the Parliament. It could come as early as October, or when the Parliament reconvenes in the spring of 1995.

We must continue our support of their demilitarization program if CWC is going to be a viable agreement among the signatory nations. This assistance makes sense because it will remove the potential direct threat to U.S. security and ensure the stockpile is not available as a temptation to potential proliferators. But the most important thing for us to do to encourage Russian ratification and implementation is for us to ratify the CWC and promptly pass the implementing legislation which is before you.

The CWC represents a great opportunity not only for the global community to ban an entire class of weapons of mass destruction, but it will also make more difficult the proliferation of those weapons throughout the Third World or to rogue states. While the CWC obviously will not preclude the possibility of CW proliferation, without it, the global community has no vehicle to address the issue. The CWC creates international norms that establish both the standards by which behavior of states can be judged and the criteria for determining appropriate actions if states are deemed to violate such standards. If states choose to ratify the CWC, they must allow both routine and challenge inspections. However, if they choose to forgo inclusion, they become increasingly isolated politically and economically from the signatory states.

THE VERIFICATION PROVISIONS OF CWC

The verification provisions of the CWC have been an item of controversy ever since the United States submitted the first comprehensive draft text to the Conference on Disarmament in Geneva. While the final product reflects the U.S. initial proposal, it does differ from any other treaty yet negotiated. It calls for intrusive on-site inspections that not only go well beyond government installations to reach private industry, but also include short notice inspections of undeclared facilities, including those that have no explicit history of actual involvement in any CW program.

The verification provisions of CWC effectively deal with the ambiguity of chemical weapons, which are not far removed in—far removed chemically from substances with important legitimate functions. In my opinion, the ratification regime contained in the CWC is the most effective ever negotiated and should serve as a model for other negotiations.

SUPPORT OF CHEMICAL MANUFACTURERS ASSOCIATION

As a world leader in the chemical industry, the United States was concerned throughout the negotiations about its cost to industry. Almost unprecedented cooperation and input from leading trade associations, particularly the CMA, have assured the provisions of the CWC have well-considered industry concerns. I want to commend Will Carpenter, a witness today, and the CMA for being a fully participating partner throughout the negotiations in reaching this milestone agreement. Without their full participation and positive cooperation, reaching agreement would have been impossible.

PROVISIONS OF IMPLEMENTING LEGISLATION

The spirit of cooperation has carried over to this Nation's internal deliberation on the content of the implementing legislation. The administration has put forward CWC implementing legislation for consideration by Congress which addresses the many concerns of industry without compromising the integrity of the convention itself. Their continued cooperation will be key to the implementation of the agreement.

The constitutional guarantees against unreasonable searches and seizures must be protected and, at the same time, we must allow searches which will have international credibility. Likewise, we must be sensitive to the concerns of industry, so their business interests and proprietary secrets are not compromised.

I believe the implementing legislation does so, but I commend to you the testimony of Mr. Carpenter with regard to the reasonableness of observer participation in the process. I am also concerned about the expansion of the definition of toxic chemicals. I believe this is not in keeping with the agreement and hope that the legislation will simply include the CWC reference to the scheduled chemicals.

Please also examine whether the $50,000 per day criminal penalties have any deterrent value in reporting minor violations and whether they will punish legitimate refusals to allow an inspection. A tiered approach to criminal penalties should be considered, to take into account the nature of the violation and make the penalty fit the crime.

Lastly, we must make certain that the legislation recognizes and respects the regulatory decisions of the Preparatory Commission and the Secretariat and protects against U.S. agency regulations which may compete with or are more onerous than those regulations from many sources.

Industry should not be required to sort out, be knowledgeable of and abide by a plethora of burdens and regulations. One U.S. agency should harmonize those regulations and guard against other regulatory schemes.

In closing, I believe the CWC presents us with an opportunity of historic proportion to implement a treaty to ban an entire species of weapons among participating nations and create safeguards against the proliferation of those weapons. I urge my colleagues to consider favorably the regulations put forward by the administration for the implementation of the CWC.

Chairman HAMILTON. Thank you very much, Mr. Lancaster. We are very grateful to you for the way you have followed this so carefully over a period of years.

BIPARTISAN SUPPORT FOR CWC

The Convention was really negotiated by the previous administration, the Bush administration, and confirmed by the Clinton administration?

Mr. LANCASTER. That is correct.

Chairman HAMILTON. Throughout this period of time, have you as a Member of Congress had good access and good cooperation with the administrations you dealt with?

Mr. LANCASTER. I did indeed. In fact, as Mr. Gilman commented, I was in Geneva on many occasions working with our representative to the talks. I had an opportunity, likewise, in Washington to meet from time to time with administration representatives; and through writings and speeches, I believe, influenced their decision on a negotiating position and moved them toward a position which was ultimately put forward and adopted in the talks.

At all times, I felt that I had full and complete access to the information I needed and to the personnel who were involved in the negotiation. At all times, they were very cooperative.

Chairman HAMILTON. This is one instance where congressional and executive branch relations worked smoothly and well?

Mr. LANCASTER. It did from my perspective, yes, Mr. Chairman.

PROSPECTS FOR SENATE RATIFICATION

Chairman HAMILTON. Where is it in the Senate, the convention? What is the schedule over there? Do you know?

Mr. LANCASTER. I cannot tell you that, Mr. Chairman.

Chairman HAMILTON. If the Senate does not ratify it before the end of the Congress, what are the consequences, do you think, of that?

Mr. LANCASTER. That simply means, in all probability, that the convention will not go into force, as now anticipated, 6 months after January of 1995. In my opinion, until the United States ratifies and passes implementing legislation, a large number of state parties to the agreement will likewise withhold ratification and implementing legislation. I believe our ratification is the key to the number of signatories necessary to enter into force.

U.S. AND RUSSIAN RATIFICATION CRITICAL

Chairman HAMILTON. It is not likely we will get the 65 we need unless the United States acts?

Mr. LANCASTER. There is no question we will not get the 65 until we act. Likewise, I think if Russia does not ratify and implement, another large segment of signatory countries will not ratify; and so I believe that it is critical for both countries to ratify and pass implementing legislation by January of 1995. Any delay in ratification simply delays the entering into force of the convention until some time next year.

Chairman HAMILTON. Mr. Gilman.

REPORTS OF RUSSIAN CHEMICAL WEAPONS PRODUCTION

Mr. GILMAN. Thank you, Mr. Chairman. Again, I thank Congressman Lancaster for his concerns and his assistance in trying to bring this to the attention of the Congress and for continuing his monitoring of this important treaty.

Mr. Lancaster, in your testimony, you indicate the most important thing for us to do is to encourage Russian ratification and implementation and to try to do it promptly. While we agree with that statement, as I indicated in my opening statement, I do have concerns about Russia's commitment to the treaty, particularly in the wake of recent disclosures that Russia has been concealing efforts to develop advanced chemical weapons.

What do we make of those disclosures? What can we do to prevent that from happening? Do you have any other concerns about Russia's commitment?

Mr. LANCASTER. Congressman Browder and I accompanied Assistant Secretary of Defense Harold Smith to Russia in January. Congressman Browder accompanied him again to Russia in July of this year. I was not able to go with them on that occasion.

I continue to have concerns about Russia's reluctance, or at least on the part of some in Russia, their reluctance to move forward in good faith to disclose not only their stockpiles but also all research efforts that they have been engaged in in the past and they may still even be as of this date.

I think the key to stopping this action is, in fact, to obtain ratification and the entering into force of the convention. Once that occurs, you will then have the mechanism by which to have routine and challenge inspections that, I think, will promptly bring any further action to a halt.

There are some old mossbacks in the Ministry of Defense in Russia that will continue to push for a chemical capability in Russia until the treaty is ratified, until it enters into force and until the first inspection; but I believe when that occurs, that will bring it to a halt.

So I think that that is why it is so important for us to push them in that direction, so that we can have the mechanism in place to guarantee that those efforts do stop.

Mr. GILMAN. What do we do about countries that don't sign this? For example, Libya, some of the other rogue countries that are out there? How do we bring about implementation of what our objectives are with those countries?

PROVISIONS FOR DEALING WITH NONSIGNATORY NATIONS

Mr. LANCASTER. Of course, the convention's provisions with regard to dealing with nonsignatory nations, I believe will be very effective in isolating those countries both economically and politically from the rest of the world. This will, for all practical purposes, eliminate any prospect of those countries having any significant chemical industry, because they simply are not going to have access to a wide range of perfectly legitimate and legal chemicals, and those which can be used in chemical weapons will not be available to them. I think that will cripple any efforts on their part to develop a chemical industry of a legitimate nature, to say nothing of chemical weapons.

Likewise, I think when a significant number—in fact, the number that has signed the treaty is truly impressive—when they have all ratified and when this goes into effect, I think that you will have only a handful of nations remaining that will not be a part of the process, and it will be much easier to isolate them both economically and politically.

LEVEL OF DEMILITARIZATION AID TO RUSSIA

Mr. GILMAN. Mr. Lancaster, what do you believe is the appropriate level of U.S. assistance to Russia to destroy their chemical weapons through the program?

Mr. LANCASTER. As Mr. Browder and Secretary Smith and I have said repeatedly in meetings both here in Washington with Russian officials and in Moscow, they simply cannot count on this country destroying their stockpiles and their manufacturing capacity, because we have that same obligation here in this country in the demilitarization of our chemical stockpiles and facilities.

I do think it is appropriate, however, to assist them with technologies, which we are doing now. A contract has been signed with the Bechtel Company to go to Russia and develop a plan of demilitarization and make recommendations to them on appropriate technologies. We are making available to the Russian Government the technologies that we have researched and have in place.

We are also providing to them the benefits of research and other technologies which we have chosen not to use in this country. We have also already made available to them assistance in setting up a laboratory to continue research and destruction and also to verify the technologies which will be proposed in the Bechtel contract; and I think that that should be the nature of our assistance.

Once they have decided on a technology and a first site for destruction, I think it would be appropriate for us to assist in the construction of that first facility. I do not think we should ever pay the full costs of any part of their demilitarization program.

COST OF RUSSIAN CW DESTRUCTION PROGRAM

Mr. GILMAN. What do you estimate to be the total costs of the implementation of this program?

Mr. LANCASTER. That is very difficult to say until the Bechtel study is completed. But it will, in fact, lay out a program of demilitarization for the Russian Government which may give us a better idea.

It also is impossible to say until the method of destruction is chosen because some methods are more or less expensive. Also, if they choose to do as we have done and destroy at each storage site, that admittedly is more expensive, but perhaps more acceptable to the public, than two or three large destruction sites to which you would transport the chemicals. That clearly would be the cheapest method and may be a method that Russia chooses.

If they choose the method that we do, then it would be more expensive. It is hard to say until they choose the method of destruction or program of destruction exactly what that cost would be.

POISON GASES NOT COVERED BY TREATY

Mr. GILMAN. Just one other question, Mr. Chairman.

Congressman Lancaster, one criticism of the treaty is that it does not cover common poison gases such as chlorine and hydrogen cyanide. Is that correct? It doesn't cover those? Why didn't the convention cover those?

Mr. LANCASTER. Mr. Gilman, I apologize, but I am not able to answer that kind of technical question. I am sure Mr. Carpenter can answer that very question when he testifies.

Mr. GILMAN. I will save that for him.

I want to thank you for your efforts.

And thank you, Mr. Chairman.

Mr. LANCASTER. Thank you.

Chairman HAMILTON. Mr. Browder.[1]

RUSSIAN RESISTANCE TO DESTRUCTION OF CHEMICALS WEAPONS

Mr. BROWDER. Thank you, Mr. Chairman. I would like to express my appreciation for being invited to participate in this hearing, and I would particularly like to congratulate Mr. Lancaster on his testi-

---

[1] Hon. Glen Browder is a Representative in Congress from the State of Alabama.

mony this morning. He has provided, like you, leadership on this issue. We are grateful to him.

I would like to probe him on a couple of points because I know he has some experience that would add to the written testimony that he has prepared this morning. I would follow up a couple of the points that Mr. Gilman has raised.

Mr. Lancaster, the Russians do not have a very good track record on destroying their chemical weapons. What is your opinion or thinking as to why they have such a poor record? Is it because they do not want to destroy them, or what?

Mr. LANCASTER. I think you have several dynamics at work here.

First of all, I think in the past it was very definitely the Ministry of Defense that was opposed to—opposed probably even to the convention, but certainly opposed to eliminating any prospect of a chemical capacity for their military, and also opposed to destruction of the facilities and the stockpiles.

I think you also have another dynamic at work. That is that since, just as in this country, chemical weapons can be produced in facilities that might be adapted for nonweapons use, you have a situation where a country is in dire economic straits who would like very much to continue to use some of those facilities by converting them to peaceful uses, something that is made very difficult by the convention.

Then, lastly, I think the most important thing right now is that they simply do not have the money. I think that that is their greatest drawback among even those who strongly support the convention, and demilitarization of their stocks and capabilities. That is why I think it is important for us to render assistance.

One of the things that I have done, which I will continue to pursue through the North Atlantic Assembly, the parliamentary arm of NATO, is a task force, which I hope will be appointed in November, which will be used to encourage other NATO countries to participate in the chemical demilitarization program in Russia, because at this point we are the only country that has rendered concrete assistance though private industry in Germany and Italy and have also proposed to be partners in the destruction process; no other governments at this point have actually contributed funds.

TIMEFRAME FOR DESTRUCTION OF RUSSIAN STOCKPILE

Mr. BROWDER. Mr. Lancaster, do you think Russia will be able to complete the destruction of its chemical weapons within the 10-year period?

Mr. LANCASTER. Not unless they move much more aggressively than they have in the past. The Convention does, of course, provide a safety valve for an extension beyond the initial period for destruction; and I would anticipate that unless there is a much more aggressive approach to demilitarization, that that extension probably will have to be granted.

Mr. BROWDER. Do you think this argues against ratification of the Chemical Weapons Convention?

Mr. LANCASTER. No, I don't think it argues against ratification. I think we must begin the process and deal with that process as it continues. As I say, it was anticipated there might be difficulties in meeting the schedule, and that is why the provisions for extension were included in the convention.

KEY RUSSIAN CONCERNS

Mr. BROWDER. Thank you. Again, I want to congratulate you for your work.

Mr. Chairman, would it be in order for me to make a point about our conversations, following up Mr. Lancaster's and my work with the members of the Russian Duma and the Russian administration this past month in which they expressed their commitment to the Chemical Weapons Convention—their strong commitment; and the key questions as a result of our work with Dr. Smith. The key questions that the Russians have expressed to us are, first, whether they want to place themselves under the clock, the Chemical Weapons Convention clock, the 10-year time limit, after the forced destruction of their stocks; and whether, second, they can financially obligate themselves because of the cost of the destruction of chemical weapons and the costs of verification.

I believe it is critical not only that we support the Chemical Weapons Convention, but that the United States be engaged with the Russians on several levels—financial, through Nunn-Lugar funds, congressional, parliamentary, technical, DOD, MOD teams and contractors.

ADDRESSING ALLEGATIONS OF SECRET RUSSIAN PROGRAM

Mr. Gilman asked about the questions—about the continued development; particularly, there was comment in the news media about a secret program that was continuing. We expressed our concerns to the Russian Government—strong concerns to the Russians about this event; and I came away from our meetings with the conclusion that this was both a fortunate and an unfortunate development. It was fortunate because it brought the issue to a head, and we were able to address it and express our concerns to them. But also I think it was unfortunate in that I don't think we will accomplish our objectives through headlines or news media stories.

What we did, since we are not in the negotiating business, we told the Russians—urged them very strongly to return to the discussion table for the bilateral discussions. I think they were receptive to that.

Thank you very much, Mr. Chairman.

Chairman HAMILTON. Mr. Browder, we appreciate the contributions you have made, as well as Mr. Lancaster, to this process. I think it has been important. You, he and others have represented the Congress, I think, with considerable distinction in working on the convention. We are grateful to you for your leadership.

Mr. Goodling.

Mr. GOODLING. Like you, Mr. Chairman, Congressman Lancaster answers all my questions between 6 and 6:30 in the morning in the gymnasium. I have no others.

Chairman HAMILTON. You have got the jump on the rest of us.

Mrs. Meyers.

Mrs. MEYERS. No questions, Mr. Chairman. I am sorry to be late. I did scan your testimony, Mr. Lancaster. I will read it more carefully. I am very pleased about your work in this area.

Mr. LANCASTER. Thank you.

Chairman HAMILTON. Thank you very much, Mr. Lancaster. We are sorry to have detained you for a while. We appreciate very much your appearance.

Chairman HAMILTON. I will ask the members of the second panel to come forward: Mr. Donald Mahley from ACDA; Dr. Will Carpenter from the Chemical Manufacturers Association; and Mr. Michael L. Moodie from the Chemical and Biological Arms Control Institute.

It doesn't make any difference to the chair who begins here. Your statements, of course, will be entered into the record in full.

Mr. Moodie.

STATEMENT OF MICHAEL L. MOODIE, PRESIDENT, CHEMICAL AND BIOLOGICAL ARMS CONTROL INSTITUTE

Mr. MOODIE. Mr. Chairman, I appreciate the opportunity to be with you to discuss the broader context within which the implementing legislation must be considered, in particular some of the concerns that have been raised about the Chemical Weapons Convention. I want to be very clear, I do not come as a critic of the convention but as a supporter and as a member of the Bush administration who was involved in concluding the negotiations of the convention.

LIMITED VALUE OF CHEMICAL WEAPONS DETERRENT

I would like to touch briefly on four issues. First, it has been argued by some of the opponents of the treaty that by forgoing chemical weapons, the United States will deny itself deterrence in kind, which could endanger both U.S. interests and U.S. forces in some situations. In my view, chemical weapons provide only a marginal contribution to deterrence, especially in light of the overwhelming conventional power the United States can bring to bear in most situations. Even if the United States retained chemical weapons, it is questionable whether the political leadership would ever make the decision to use them.

During the Gulf war, Saddam Hussein was clearly deterred from using his extensive chemical stockpile. No one knows for sure why he did, but a number of explanations have been offered, including that he believed that if he used chemical weapons, coalition war aims would shift from removing Iraq from Kuwait to removing Saddam from Baghdad. To my mind, these explanations are more plausible reasons for Saddam Hussein's decision not to use chemical weapons than the prospect of CW retaliation.

VERIFICATION

The second concern is the argument that the CWC is not verifiable. If one's standard of verification is 100 percent certainty that any violation would be detected, then the CWC is not verifiable. It will not uncover in every case a smoking gun that provides incontrovertible evidence of a violation.

But verification is not some mechanistic process. It is a process of making judgments about information, only some of which is derived from treaty-defined procedures and some of which is generated from other sources, including technical and human intelligence. This information creates a mosaic of a state's compliance behavior. If a piece does not seem to fit that mosaic, then more intense scrutiny can be directed at the state in question.

Development of a militarily significant chemical weapons program is not a small, isolated activity. It includes many stages—research and development; production in amounts that can make a difference on the battlefield; storage of tons, if not thousands, of tons of agent; munitions filling; training and so on.

Some of these activities are more detectable than others. By banning all of them, the CWC creates the opportunity to identify a range of possible irregularities in a state's behavior if that state is indeed attempting covert CW proliferation.

A second point about verification: During the negotiations, enormous time and effort were devoted to achieving an acceptable balance between two competing but equall valid objectives, one, intrusiveness of on-site inspections neededyto ensure the treaty's objectives are being met; and, two, limitations on that intrusiveness to protect vital national security and confidential business information.

Both of these objectives are important national interests, and one should not be pursued at the expense of the other.

THE SITUATION IN RUSSIA

A third concern which has already come up this morning is the situation in Russia, the repository of the world's largest declared chemical weapons stockpile. The United States has bilateral agreements with the Russian Federation designed to create greater openness about each side's CW-related practices.

The administration has voiced concerns about how forthcoming the Russians have been in providing the required information under the terms of this agreement. I understand, however—and Don Mahley can speak to this more directly in the questions—that the administration is currently seeking clarifications of those particular aspects of the Russian data that are felt to be incomplete or inaccurate.

This leads to the more general question about what the Russians are doing in the chemical weapons area and the charges that they are engaged in research on binary chemical weapons. It should be pointed out, under the current international regime, there is nothing illegal about such activity. The 1925 Geneva protocol does not prohibit research on and even production of chemical weapons, only their use. It is only when the Chemical Weapons Convention enters into force that such activity would no longer be allowed.

No one who does not have access to classified information can be certain of the accuracy of these charges. In some cases, for example, the charges have been made by Russians whose involvement in the alleged activities occurred several years ago. Whether there is more recent evidence of such activity is a question for representatives from the intelligence community.

There are, though, competing explanations for the way the Russians have been behaving, not just that Moscow is up to something nefarious. The Russian Government is a government in transition and, as such, it suffers from shoddy, sloppy work. Some of the problems with the information exchanged under the bilateral agreement may be the result of confusion and inefficiency that currently prevail throughout the bureaucracy in Moscow.

Alternatively, we might be seeing the results of bureaucratic competition, not over the direction of policy, but over the control of resources.

Elements of the Russian bureaucracy throughout the government are involved in an intense competition for very scarce resources, and the difficulties that have been encountered could reflect a fight for control over CW-related money.

Everything the Russians have said about their compliance with the CWC has been linked to resources which they do not have. The Duma has made it clear it will not ratify the CWC until it has an implementation plan, a crucial aspect of which will be funding.

Current Russian behavior may be an attempt to leverage additional resources from Washington and other countries keenly interested in getting the Russians on board the CWC as quickly as possible. The Congress is likely to be confronted with requests for additional assistance to Russia to facilitate chemical weapons destruction and other aspects of CWC implementation. In my view, such assistance could prove to be crucial in ensuring that Russia is able to meet the time lines for CW destruction outlined in the treaty.

At the same time, the Russians must be reminded that the obligations under the treaty are theirs, and they must demonstrate the requisite commitment to meeting the CWC's objectives. Sending this message loud and clear in your exchanges with your Russian parliamentary counterparts could prove extremely valuable.

In general, I would urge our operating assumption to be that the expressed commitments of the senior Russian leadership to the CWC and its objectives are genuine, but we should obviously continue to watch the situation in Russia carefully. At the same time, we should remember the comments of JCS Chairman General Shalikashvili and CIA Director Woolsey that ratification and entry into force of the CWC is in the interests of the United States, whatever the situation in Russia.

NEED FOR CONTINUED DETERRENT MEASURES

The final concern I would mention, Mr. Chairman, is a warning against complacency. The CWC is not a panacea for the problem of chemical weapons proliferation. It is only one of several policy tools that must be utilized.

The CWC will not obviate the need for a robust, adequately funded chemical defense program. National intelligence capabilities will remain crucial; so, too, will maintaining an effective deterrent through conventional forces. Only if the CWC works together effectively with these other policy tools will the United States and the members of the international community meet the challenge of chemical weapons successfully.

Thank you very much.

Chairman HAMILTON. Thank you very much, Mr. Moodie.

Mr. Mahley, we have your statement. It is in the record in full. We would appreciate your summary of it.

STATEMENT OF DONALD MAHLEY, ACTING ASSISTANT DIRECTOR OF MULTILATERAL AFFAIRS, U.S. ARMS CONTROL AND DISARMAMENT AGENCY

Mr. MAHLEY. I appreciate the opportunity to come here today to testify before you on the implementing legislation. I would, of course, apologize for my Director, John Holum, Director of the Arms Control and Disarmament Agency, who unfortunately could not be here today, but is in Geneva right now meeting with the heads of delegations of the Ad Hoc Committee on a Nuclear Test Ban to underscore the President's commitment to achieving that test ban at the earliest possible time.

COMMENDATION OF REPRESENTATIVES LANCASTER, BROWDER AND PORTER

At the outset, I would like to express appreciation for your leadership in introducing H.R. 4849, the administration's proposed Chemical Weapons Convention Implementing Act of 1994. We also greatly appreciate the bipartisan support for this legislation as reflected in the participation of Representatives Berman, Gilman, Lantos, Oxley and Swift in that introduction. We appreciate the ability to discuss the implementation of the CWC.

In examining the congressional role in arms control treaties, most people look to the U.S. Senate. I would like to take a moment to give credit with respect to the CWC, where it is also due—here, to the House side of the U.S. Congress.

One of your colleagues, Representative Martin Lancaster, who testified earlier, is deserving of special recognition. He has indeed played a key role in the progress we have made to date in achieving the Chemical Weapons Convention and moving toward bringing it into force. His expertise on the convention and the issues it contains, his active participation both here and at the negotiations in Geneva, have helped us get a convention that meets all interests involved. His work with the Russians has spurred their efforts to meet their commitments, and his work in Washington has broadened and increased understanding and support for the convention.

In addition to his work there, the unflagging attention of this committee and the efforts of the House Arms Control Observers group have been constructive in supporting this negotiation over the years. The contributions of Representatives Glen Browder and John Porter, both in furthering chemical weapons defensive preparedness and in support of this treaty, have indeed been most useful.

BIPARTISAN SUPPORT FOR CWC

Thank you, sir; and let me turn to this morning's topic: implementation of the Chemical Weapons Convention.

In your invitation to us to testify, you requested we address the significance to other countries of U.S. ratification, the importance of the convention to U.S. nonproliferation objectives, the effectiveness in halting CW proliferation, the verifiability of the CWC, and, finally, my Agency's position on the draft implementing legislation.

Mr. Chairman, the CWC culminates years of bipartisan efforts to ban chemical weapons globally. Then-Vice President George Bush, as you know, submitted a draft text of the CW Convention to the Conference on Disarmament in Geneva back on April 18, 1984. It was negotiated under President Reagan, concluded and signed by President Bush, and submitted to the Senate for ratification under President Clinton.

U.S. LEADERSHIP ROLE

To date, 157 countries have signed the convention. Nine countries have thus far ratified. Nearly three-fourths of the countries believed to possess or to be seeking to acquire chemical weapons have signed the Chemical Weapons Convention.

In his address to the United Nations General Assembly last fall, President Clinton called upon all countries—including our own—to ratify the Chemical Weapons Convention as quickly as possible so it could enter into force at the earliest possible date. Throughout the negotiations and subsequent to the conclusion of the convention, other countries have looked to the United States for leadership. We shepherded the convention through the U.N. endorsement process and through the signing ceremony in Paris and have been active in the Preparatory Commission in The Hague. Our leadership role continues through our ratification efforts. Many countries, as Representative Lancaster stated earlier today, are looking toward the United States for leadership in that ratification effort.

On submitting the Chemical Weapons Convention to the Senate on November 23, 1993, President Clinton stated this convention is a central element of his nonproliferation policy and will significantly enhance U.S. national security and contribute to greater global security.

WHAT THE CWC DOES

The Chemical Weapons Convention is both a disarmament and nonproliferation treaty. It addresses the demand for and the supply of chemical weapons. It requires parties to destroy their chemical weapons and chemical weapons production facilities and to open their chemical industries to international inspection. It prohibits parties from transferring chemical weapons to others or from assisting any other nation in any other activity prohibited by the convention. States that are parties to the convention must ban trade in specified chemicals with countries that decline to join the convention. These nonproliferation provisions serve as a disincentive for staying outside the regime.

Moreover, the Chemical Weapons Convention will establish a new international norm that will serve as a basis for applying international pressure against nonparties who already possess or are attempting to acquire chemical weapons.

VERIFIABILITY OF PROVISIONS OF CWC

Mr. Chairman, you have asked us whether the Chemical Weapons Convention is verifiable. The administration has determined the convention has achieved the standard of being effectively verifiable and that it will protect and enhance our national security assets and interests. The net effect of the provisions will increase the risk of detection and the political price of noncompliance and thus serve to deter potential CWC violators. This conclusion is reflected in the verification report required by section 37 of the Arms Control and Disarmament Act submitted to the Senate as a consensus report of executive branch agencies and the intelligence community.

During the negotiations, the United States sought to protect U.S. proprietary concerns, constitutional rights and national security while at the same time providing sufficient access to relevant facilities to ensure effective verification and deterrence. Both the Bush and Clinton administrations and the U.S. chemical industry were satisfied that in the end the final balance of the convention was adequate to both provide those sufficient provisions to safeguard that which needs protecting and to address compliance concerns so as to be able to investigate those things that need to be investigated.

INVOLVEMENT OF U.S. CHEMICAL INDUSTRY

The Chemical Weapons Convention contains a number of provisions that require implementing legislation to give them effect within the United States. Accordingly, the administration drafted and submitted to the Congress its proposed act, which your committee has now introduced. This draft legislation reflects comments by industry—specifically the Chemical Manufacturers Association—and several other industry associations, the staff of relevant congressional committees, and academic experts. In addition, it relies as much on legislative precedent as possible. For example, the criminal prohibitions were drawn from the Biological Weapons Antiterrorism Act, and many of the declaration and inspection provisions were drawn from the Toxic Substances Control Act.

While noting some areas need further work, industry's overall reaction to the proposed act—as I am sure you will hear in greater detail in a moment, from Mr. Carpenter—has been very favorable. The Chemical Manufacturers Association, in particular, has stressed the importance to industry of the act's strong protections against disclosure of information, its declared policy of taking the competitive impact on industry into account during U.S. implementation of the Chemical Weapons Convention and its input into facility agreements governing inspections of chemical facilities.

In conclusion, Mr. Chairman, our lawyers have worked closely with congressional staffers to explain the relationship between provisions of the CWC and the proposed implementing legislation and to ensure that all concerns were addressed. We look forward to a continued, close working relationship as we endeavor to craft legislation that meets the obligations of the Chemical Weapons Convention and serves to protect the United States' national interests.

Thank you, Mr. Chairman.

[The prepared statement of Mr. Mahley appears at the conclusion of the hearing.]

Chairman HAMILTON. Mr. Carpenter.

STATEMENT OF WILL CARPENTER, VICE CHAIRMAN OF THE BOARD, AGRIDYNE TECHNOLOGIES, INC., AND CHAIRMAN, CHEMICAL MANUFACTURERS ASSOCIATION WORKING GROUP ON CHEMICAL WEAPONS

Mr. CARPENTER. Thank you, Mr. Chairman. I appreciate the opportunity to be here on behalf of the Chemical Manufacturers Association.

CMA SUPPORTS CWC

Our message to the committee today is straightforward. CMA strongly supports the Chemical Weapons Convention. And we strongly support effective, efficient and practical measures to implement the convention. Your hearing today is a means of assuring that we meet the challenge of complete CWC implementation.

If I might add, there is a sequence of history, logic and fact that absolutely dictates that the chemical industry participate and indeed be a resource in what has taken place over the last 15 years. Chemical weapons being produced in 1916 quite effectively means that there is a wide range of chemical industry facilities around the world that are quite capable, given a government's decision, of making chemical weapons. Therefore, in order for our treaty to be verifiable, the chemical industry of every country must be brought in under that treaty.

Given that fact, then it is obvious that the chemical industry itself must be a resource in the education and understanding of how that can be achieved.

Before I delve into the specifics, I want to make special mention also of the commitment and leadership demonstrated by Martin Lancaster to the goal of eradicating chemical weapons. He is Congress' true expert on the CWC, and he has devoted a great deal of time and attention to making sure that the CWC is a good deal for the United States. He has tracked the thorny issues in chemical arms control; he has tracked the particular problem of the Russian CW stocks. The CWC is in no small part a result of his commitment.

We would also not be here today without the hard work of Don Mahley and the negotiators at the U.S. Arms Control and Disarmament Agency. We would not be here today if you, Mr. Chairman, had not committed valuable resources in tracking the CWC. And from my point of view, we would not be here today were it not for my industry's conviction that chemical weapons can be eliminated.

VERIFIABILITY OF CWC

The CWC is, in our view, a verifiable convention.

Our conviction springs from a belief that with the chemical industry as a partner we could develop a new arms control mechanism that addressed both national security concerns and the needs of commercial interests. We think the treaty achieves those objectives. Our goal now is to assure that those principles are reflected in U.S. law.

One of our industry's goals in the ongoing implementation process is to assure that the CWC remains an arms control agreement. It was not conceived as a means of serving other policy goals, or as a means of expanding the regulatory reach over the commercial industry. CMA helped develop the CWC verification system at the multilateral level, and we need your committee's attention to making sure that system is exactly what is delivered in the United States.

Make no mistake about it. The CWC will impact the chemical industry. No other arms control agreement in history cuts so broadly and deeply into U.S. commerce. An unprecedented number of companies will be required to report their activities to the U.S. Government. Commercial facilities will be required to open their doors to on-site inspections by an international agency, on a scale never before imagined.

The challenge is to get it right the first time. We need not repeat the regulatory mistakes we have witnessed in so many other areas.

INDUSTRY INVOLVED IN CRAFTING IMPLEMENTING LEGISLATION

The implementing legislation crafted by the Clinton administration is a good step in the right direction. I am pleased to say that the administration involved the industry in drafting their proposal, and the bill addresses most of our concerns.

No other legislation, to my knowledge, expresses a need to consider regulatory burden to the degree the CWC legislation does. The significant protections for legitimate commercial interests contained in the CWC can be fairly translated into U.S. law through this legislation.

I might say I cannot remember the chemical industry ever coming before a body of Congress in such complete agreement with a proposed bill for our own regulation as in this case. So the points where we have concern, important as they are, are minor compared to the other aspects of the treaty and the legislation.

The administration took pains to mirror the CWC in drafting this legislation. The definitions contained in the legislation should not be generalized in a manner which broaden coverage of chemicals beyond that intended by the CWC.

The CWC permits the host government to be present during international inspections. In general, CMA believes that U.S. representatives can act as intermediaries between the inspected facility and the inspection team. The legislation should make clear the intention that the representatives are members of either the lead agency or the national authority. CMA recommends that the extent to which U.S. representatives participate in inspection be limited.

The legislation does not make a commitment to adopt the Preparatory Commission's regulatory decisions as part of the U.S. regulatory regime. These regulatory decisions include matters such as declaration formats, inspection procedures, and possible exemptions for certain commercial activities, such as polymers and hydrocarbon facilities. If we are to meet the policy goal suggested in the legislation of reducing the burden and competitive impact of the CWC, the U.S. regulatory system must be no more burdensome than that implemented by other Parties to the convention.

Mr. Chairman, thank you again for the opportunity to testify today. As always, we are prepared to make available whatever assistance we can to you or your staff as this historic legislation is considered.

I would be happy to answer any questions the committee might have.

[The prepared statement of Mr. Carpenter appears at the conclusion of the hearing.]

CONVENTION STRENGTHENS INTERNATIONAL NONPROLIFERATION NORMS

Chairman HAMILTON. Thank you very much, gentlemen.

Just give me in a word or two why this convention is, in your words, "in the U.S. national interests." For a good television sound bite. Not to exceed 30 seconds.

If you put it in a sentence or two, why is it in the U.S. national interests?

Mr. MAHLEY. Mr. Chairman, I will try to start out on that line.

I believe that the overwhelming reason it is in the U.S.' national interest is that it establishes, once and for all, an international norm that prohibits all of the activities associated with chemical weapons, a decision which we have taken as a national policy already, to get ourselves out of the chemical weapons business.

Mr. MOODIE. I would also add, Mr. Chairman, by doing so, it reinforces the international norm against nonproliferation more generally.

It is not just chemical weapons that are the problem. There are other things out there. I think by having the CWC on the books as part of an international legal regime against nonproliferation, the U.S. interests are served more broadly than just attacking the chemical weapons problem.

NONSIGNATORY POSSESSOR STATES

Chairman HAMILTON. With regard to the nonproliferation objectives, we have certain countries who are suspected of having chemical weapons that did not join the convention; is that correct?

What are those countries?

Mr. MAHLEY. Sir, can I take that question for the record and check with the intelligence community about what specifics we can provide?

Chairman HAMILTON. Sure.[2]

Mr. MOODIE. Mr. Chairman, I am not in the government. I can reference the open literature that exists of suspected countries with chemical weapons. That would include countries like Libya, North Korea, Syria.

Chairman HAMILTON. And Iraq.

Mr. MOODIE. Iraq has not signed the convention.

STATUS OF RATIFICATION EFFORT

Chairman HAMILTON. How many states have signed it?

Mr. MAHLEY. 157 as of today, sir.

Chairman HAMILTON. How many have ratified?

Mr. MAHLEY. Nine as of today.

Chairman HAMILTON. Why so few?

---

[2] The information requested was submitted in classified form and is retained in the committee's files.

Mr. MAHLEY. The ratification process, sir, is a long and complicated one in a number of areas. Although we have made a number of diplomatic representations to over 100 of these countries, asking them to encourage and speed up the ratification process, they are wending their way through a number of legislative and parliamentary processes, the same as we are wending our way.

I think if you go back to Representative Lancaster's statement earlier today, I would merely echo it, sir; that is that it is also the case there are—a number of these countries have indicated to us in diplomatic exchanges, as well as in statements to me as the U.S. representative to the Preparatory Commission, that they are awaiting the leadership of the United States to ensure that we have ratified the convention before they are going to take the final step.

Chairman HAMILTON. If we ratify, do you expect a stream of ratifications to come forward?

Mr. MAHLEY. That is correct, sir.

PROSPECTS FOR U.S. RATIFICATION

Chairman HAMILTON. What is your prediction about ratification, assuming the Senate ratifies this fall?

Mr. MAHLEY. In terms of getting the 65 ratifications into force? If the Senate ratifies before it recesses this fall, it is my judgment we will be able to obtain the 65 ratifications necessary to start the 180-day countdown to entry into force no later than January or February next year, 1995. If the United States fails to do that, then it is my considered personal judgment it will be unlikely that we will be able to get those 65 ratifications any time in 1995.

Mr. MOODIE. I agree with that.

Chairman HAMILTON. So the Senate ratification is very critical?

Mr. MOODIE. Yes, sir.

Mr. MAHLEY. Yes, sir.

Chairman HAMILTON. When do you think the Senate will act? Do you have information on that?

Mr. MAHLEY. The only thing I can tell you on that, sir, is at the last Senate Foreign Relations Committee hearing which was held last month, Senator Pell at that hearing indicated he believed the Senate Foreign Relations Committee had concluded its hearings. I have been in contact with some members of his staff who indicated the Senate Foreign Relations Committee is now preparing a report on the ratification issue.

The Senate Select Committee on Intelligence has also indicated that they have concluded their hearings and are now in the process of drafting their report on the issue.

The Senate Armed Services Committee has still not held hearings on the matter, sir.

Chairman HAMILTON. Do you know of significant opposition in the Senate?

Mr. MAHLEY. No, I do not, sir.

PROSPECTS FOR RUSSIAN RATIFICATION

Chairman HAMILTON. Where does Russian ratification stand?

Mr. MAHLEY. Russian ratification at the moment, sir, is that the resolution of ratification was introduced last year—I am sorry, earlier this year—into the Duma, the Russian Parliament. At the moment, the Duma is not in session. Likewise, at the moment, that resolution of ratification is lying dormant. I have no information about when the Duma has scheduled another set of hearings or any further action.

Chairman HAMILTON. You have no expectation as to when they will complete action then?

Mr. MAHLEY. No, sir.

I would go back to the statement by Mr. Browder and by Mr. Lancaster earlier today and simply agree with that; it is my view and what we have heard from the Russians that one of the major concerns of the Russian Duma is making sure they have the resources available to implement the convention and that the Russian executive branch, if you will, can provide them with those assurances before they are going to be prepared to act on ratification.

The executive branch was due to and did, to the best of my knowledge, submit on the 30th of June to the Duma a new, revised plan for the destruction of Russian chemical weapons. That has not been, to my knowledge, considered by the Duma yet; and, therefore, I think that that is still in the "to be studied" category.

Mr. BROWDER. If the gentleman will yield, Mr. Chairman, we met with some of the Duma members last month. They told us they plan to hold hearings on that revised plan, this entire issue this fall. We will be meeting with some of those same members tomorrow afternoon to discuss this issue.

Chairman HAMILTON. Do you think the Duma is waiting for the United States to act? The Senate.

Mr. MAHLEY. The Duma comes back into session in October. Although I have not talked to any Duma members, I think, if the United States has completed ratification at that point, it would be a very important—at least for me, as the U.S. representative at the Preparatory Commission, speaking to the Russian delegations there, a very important lever to be able to put to the Duma and the Russian Government that we had completed that action.

Mr. MOODIE. Mr. Chairman, if I might, in informal conversations with Russian representatives, they have often suggested that their ratification process is in phase with ours, if somewhat behind ours. I think, as Mr. Mahley has suggested, if the U.S. Senate has ratified, then the pressure really will be on the Duma to move. Sometimes I think the Russians are a little bit optimistic in terms of their representation of their process.

REPORTS OF RUSSIAN CHEMICAL WEAPONS REPRODUCTION

Chairman HAMILTON. Is Russia continuing to produce chemical weapons?

Mr. MAHLEY. Sir, we have no indication that at the moment there is an active production process for chemical weapons in the Russian Federation.

Chairman HAMILTON. Do we disclose, exchange information with the Russians with regard to chemical weapons?

Mr. MAHLEY. Yes, sir, under the 1989 Wyoming MOU, we exchange information about production and inventors.

Chairman HAMILTON. We are satisfied they are cooperating fully?

Mr. MAHLEY. We have serious questions about some of the data. I have requested through the U.S. Embassy in Moscow some urgent consultations with the Russians to try to sort out the issues on that data exchange. I think that we can characterize—as Mr. Moodie indicated—the nature of that data exchange in a number of different ways. There are some areas which probably represent simply sloppiness, speed, haste in trying to get the information together—inconsistencies which occur, as you well know, any time you are trying to put together detailed reports.

Chairman HAMILTON. Do you have any reason to believe they are concealing information?

Mr. MAHLEY. There are reports that indicate some things which are generically not included in their data. That is why we wanted to get a consultation so we can stare them in the face and find out what their reactions are.

Chairman HAMILTON. Do you have any reason to think they are concealing information?

Mr. MAHLEY. At this time, no, sir.

RUSSIAN CHEMICAL WEAPONS DESTRUCTION PROGRAM

Chairman HAMILTON. Are they destroying chemical weapons?

Mr. MAHLEY. They have no active destruction program right now for chemical weapons.

Chairman HAMILTON. Why not?

Mr. MAHLEY. The only effort the Russians made in constructing a destruction facility was at a place called Chapoyersk. Because of environmental reasons, that was not allowed to operate. The Russians have no construction in Russia of a structure for destroying chemical weapons.

Chairman HAMILTON. We have $55 million requested for destruction of chemical weapons in Russia. What is going on there?

Mr. MAHLEY. I will be happy to get you details from the Defense Department, which is administering the program; but that program is for a planning project.

Twenty-five million dollars has been obligated. That is to provide a planning corporation, if you will, or overview to be able to bring together the various elements of the Russian program and put it together as a comprehensive plan to provide engineering data, time lines, to provide the capability to be able to let the Russians themselves analyze the resource requirements for completing their destruction program in a timeframe required by the convention.

[The information follows:]

The United States is providing technical assistance to Russia on some aspects of their CW destruction effort. Through the Nunn-Lugar Cooperative Threat Reduction Program, we have already identified up to $55 million to support Russian chemical weapons destruction. Of this total, up to $30 million could go to equip a centrally located CW laboratory in Russia. This facility would develop analytical methods and quality-control measures, conduct environmental studies, and train scientists and technicians.

On May 19, 1994, DoD awarded a contract to Bechtel Corporation for more than $7 million to assist the Russians in developing their CW destruction plan. We are currently considering other means to help the Russian CW destruction effort, including the feasibility of providing funds to assist in the construction of a CW destruction facility in Russia.

SLOW EXPENDITURE OF NUNN-LUGAR FUNDS

Chairman HAMILTON. Why has so little of that money been expended?

Mr. MAHLEY. Part of that is because we have had to sit down with the Russians and get all of the parameters of the kind of a planning project that we were going to be engaged in, negotiate with the Russians before we could let the U.S.—the contract to a U.S. contractor to be able to do that. The contract was let only recently.

Mr. MOODIE. I think also, Mr. Chairman, to be fair, the Nunn-Lugar program, has evolved to the point where some people would characterize it as a defense acquisition program, subject to all of the difficulties, regulations, and details that making decisions in the defense acquisition process are subject to. That might be a contributing factor to the slow nature of the money being expended.

Chairman HAMILTON. What do you mean by that? Our bureaucratic system?

Mr. MOODIE. Yes, sir. I think the regulations of the Defense Department cover decisions with respect to Nunn-Lugar.

Chairman HAMILTON. Are you saying the Defense Department is slow implementing this program?

Mr. MOODIE. I think there have been occasions where the process took longer than it might.

Chairman HAMILTON. So the Defense Department is slow implementing it?

Mr. MOODIE. Yes, sir.

Chairman HAMILTON. Mr. Mahley, do you agree with that?

Mr. MAHLEY. Sir, I prefer to have the Defense Department give you the answer to that one.

DELAYS ON RUSSIAN SIDE

Mr. BROWDER. Mr. Chairman, may I probe that question?

Chairman HAMILTON. Sure.

Mr. BROWDER. I think Mr. Moodie and Mr. Mahley may be able to add a little more. I think our experience has been that not only have we perhaps been a little slow with our bureaucracy, but we have had a problem also with the Russians.

We have—back in January, Congressman Lancaster and I spent almost an entire week trying to find somebody in the foreign ministry or their ministry of defense. We went all over town trying to find somebody to sign our agreement; and there is disarray on their end that contributed to it. It was only when we said we were going to come back home and suggest these Nunn-Lugar funds be spent elsewhere that we got the signature on the bottom line.

Mr. MOODIE. Sir, I think you are entirely correct. I did not want to leave the impression the fault was that of the U.S. Department of Defense. There are a lot of problems on the Russian side that contributed to this as well.

Somehow, on both sides, those problems have to get sorted out so things can move. It should not take, for example, as long as it has for the agreement on constructing a Russian laboratory to move forward.

Mr. BROWDER. Would you agree those problems are getting straightened out now?

Mr. MOODIE. Yes, sir.

REASONS FOR CHEMICAL INDUSTRY SUPPORT

Chairman HAMILTON. Thank you.

Mr. Carpenter, why is this agreement in the interests of the U.S. chemical industry?

Mr. CARPENTER. Well, first of all, Mr. Chairman, if it is to the interests of our Government, to have a chemical weapons treaty in our national policy; then, obviously, it is to ours. But from a selfish standpoint, if the U.S. industry can be assured that there is a method in place to eliminate chemical weapons, then down the road, the cloud of suspicion or concern can be lifted from the chemical industry.

Too often we end up suffering from an issue that is out there for which there is no good solution. The CWC represents a solution that will allow a level playing field in trade and enable us hopefully to do a better job of running our businesses when we have a procedure in place to ensure that our products and our processes are not used for some illegitimate purpose.

INDUSTRY VIEWS ON INSPECTION PROCESS

Chairman HAMILTON. Well, tell me about this inspection process. This is a fairly intrusive inspection process, right?

Mr. CARPENTER. Yes, sir.

Chairman HAMILTON. If somebody wants to come in and look at one of your plants, they can do that; is that right?

Mr. CARPENTER. Yes, sir.

Chairman HAMILTON. You are willing to accept that?

Mr. CARPENTER. It isn't something you get up in the morning and feel pleased about.

Chairman HAMILTON. Why do you do it?

Mr. CARPENTER. If the treaty is to do what it is set up to do— and that is, to prevent rogue nations from making chemical weapons or using chemical weapons—the only way you can do that is to have a procedure that is intrusive enough and opportunistic enough that it will deter those people from doing something that the treaty prohibits. So if you want it tough with them, by definition, it has to be tough across the board. You cannot have a treaty that says, gee, whiz, we will not be so rough on the U.S. industry; but sure as hell, we want to be tough on Iraq, Syria, and Libya.

So we think we have hit an appropriate balance in having it intrusive enough to serve its purpose and yet there are safeguards built in that we think are adequate to protect our intellectual property, our confidential business information.

I might add, Mr. Chairman, in terms of risks to industry, when you look at the fact that probably there are going to be somewhere between 5,000 and 10,000 facilities in the United States that theoretically are subject to inspection, and yet the—my best bet is that in actual fact there will be maybe 20, 30, 40 inspections in a year, for U.S. civilian industry, statistically it is a pretty low risk. The biggest risk we have is the submission of the data, our production capacities, production rates, our changes that end up going into the reporting system, that represents a bigger risk. But, there, too, we think appropriate safeguards have been built in and are possible.

TRIAL FACILITY INSPECTIONS

Mr. BROWDER. Excuse me, Mr. Carpenter. I understand that some—I am speaking of something I am not fully aware of here—but I understand that some test runs have been done on the inspections in the United States?

Mr. CARPENTER. Yes, sir.

Mr. BROWDER. We do have some feedback based on those test runs; am I correct?

Mr. CARPENTER. Yes.

Mr. BROWDER. Could you discuss that?

Mr. CARPENTER. In cooperation with ACDA, we have set up what we call trial inspections of all types at a number of facilities of all different sizes around the country.

Specifically, my company had a mock challenge inspection at our Louisiana facility, and in addition, this was done in cooperation with government-civilian-industry people in countries around the world. All of those experiences have been shared. As a result of those experiences, the procedures have been modified and changed to once again maintain the original purpose, find out if someone is in violation of a convention, and at the same time, building in safeguards. But those trial inspections and more informal visits to our facilities have taken place over the last 14 years.

Mr. BROWDER. Those trial inspections did not care about this process?

Mr. CARPENTER. Well, I think we learned a great deal from them. We learned, first of all, that they can be very burdensome on a facility that is being inspected. In other words, when you have a host of people descending on you—not only a national team, but the national authority accompanying them—it demands full-fledged attention from the plant manager and a whole host of other people.

RISK TO CONFIDENTIALITY OF PRODUCTION INFORMATION

There is some risk, of course, of losing confidential production information. But we think that that risk has been lowered, and quite frankly, in many cases, that risk has probably been overblown. If I am a country and I want to find out a secret at a facility in the United States, rather than going through the complicated task of, firsthand, getting an inspection there, getting an inspector who is willing to be crooked, getting that inspector in the right place in the facility to pick up the information—you know, you can do it that way, but my assessment is you could get somebody to hang out at the local bar near the plant and pick up probably more information a lot cheaper than you can going through that convoluted procedure.

But nevertheless, the risk is there.

Mr. BROWDER. Thank you.

Thank you, Mr. Chairman.

INSPECTION PROCEDURE TRIGGERED BY RATIFICATION

Chairman HAMILTON. Once the 65 states ratify, is that what kicks in the inspection procedure? You have to have the 65 ratify? And then——

Mr. MOODIE. Six months after 65 nations ratify the convention, the provisions of the treaty go into effect.

Chairman HAMILTON. They can inspect facilities in all countries, then, that have ratified at that point?

Mr. MAHLEY. That is correct, sir.

Chairman HAMILTON. And only countries that have ratified?

Mr. MAHLEY. Yes, sir, only countries that ratified.

Chairman HAMILTON. They cannot inspect countries that have not ratified?

Mr. MAHLEY. That is correct.

ROUTINE INSPECTION PROCEDURE

Chairman HAMILTON. There is a routine inspection and a challenge inspection; is that right?

Mr. MAHLEY. Yes, sir.

Chairman HAMILTON. What is routine?

Mr. MAHLEY. That is an inspection of a declared facility on a scheduled or semischeduled basis that takes place on the basis of a facility agreement to confirm declarations and investigate the activities of that plant to make sure they are consistent with what they say they are doing.

Chairman HAMILTON. What does that mean? Does every plant in the United States get a routine inspection then?

Mr. MAHLEY. It means then those plants in the United States or those facilities in the United States that are doing things that are declarable become subject to those kind of inspections. It does not mean that every declared facility is automatically inspected on an annual basis.

Chairman HAMILTON. How many inspectors will we have?

Mr. MAHLEY. At the moment, the personnel list for the OPCW for inspectors—and I won't guarantee you the exact accuracy of this figure—but it is somewhere around 286.

Chairman HAMILTON. Inspectors.

Mr. MAHLEY. Yes, sir.

Chairman HAMILTON. And how do they decide whether they are going to give a particular plant an inspection or not?

Mr. MAHLEY. On a routine basis?

Chairman HAMILTON. On a routine basis. We are talking about routine inspections.

Mr. MAHLEY. They will determine that on the basis of their own random selection from the number of things that they have got and the inputs of declared facilities, things of interest.

Chairman HAMILTON. What does that mean? They flip a coin?

Mr. MAHLEY. It is going to mean there will be some flipping engaged in it. On the other hand, the probability will go up, for example, that there will be more inspections in the United States than somewhere like India.

NUMBER OF PLANTS SUBJECT TO INSPECTION

Chairman HAMILTON. How many plants in the United States are subject to inspection?

Mr. CARPENTER. A range of 5,000 to 10,000.

Chairman HAMILTON. How many plants are subject to inspection if all the countries ratify?

Mr. MAHLEY. One of the things, sir, we don't know but I would give you a ball-park estimate of probably somewhere between 40,000 and 45,000 around the world.

Chairman HAMILTON. Plants.

Mr. MAHLEY. Yes, sir.

Chairman HAMILTON. Chemical plants.

OK. That is routine now.

You have a challenge inspection, too. What does that mean?

Mr. MAHLEY. That, sir, is an inspection which is a short notice inspection that may be at a declared or undeclared facility. So the number of facilities you have declared is not material to that. A challenge inspection can go anywhere. It is something that a state party must specifically request and it must request it of the international organization on the basis of an expressed concern with compliance with the convention.

PROCEDURE FOR LAUNCHING A CHALLENGE INSPECTION

Chairman HAMILTON. So, we have a suspicion that a country is producing chemical weapons? What do we do?

Mr. MAHLEY. What we would do—just to give you a hypothetical example is get our own information that led us to believe a country was violating a provision of the convention, say, producing chemical weapons. We would gather that information, determine which of that information was declassified or downgradeable enough from the sensitivity category. We could share that as a basis for our challenge with the international organization to, in essence, educate their inspectors about what they ought to be going in to look for. We would provide that to the Director-General of the organization in The Hague, who would organize and dispatch the challenge inspection team. They would go, then, on the basis of our information to the country which we challenged, ask to go in, when they got there, to that specific facility, and go in and conduct the challenge inspection.

Chairman HAMILTON. What if the challenge inspection is frivolous?

Mr. MOODIE. There is a provision within the treaty, Mr. Chairman, for stopping an inspection by vote of the executive council of the international organization.

Chairman HAMILTON. Who is on this executive council?

Mr. MOODIE. The executive council is composed of 41 of those states who have ratified the treaty.

Chairman HAMILTON. Are we on it?

Mr. MOODIE. There is a complicated formula that does not specify the United States; but given the nature of the formula, it is likely the United States will serve on the executive committee on a continuing basis.

INSPECTION PROCEDURE PROTECTS U.S. INTERESTS

Chairman HAMILTON. In any event, all of you are satisfied that the inspection provisions, both routine and challenge, are satisfactory and fully protect the interests of the United States and fully protect the interests of the chemical companies of this country; is that correct?

Mr. CARPENTER. Yes, sir.

Mr. MOODIE. Yes, sir.

Mr. MAHLEY. We are confident that we have gotten the correct balance to do that, yes, sir.

Chairman HAMILTON. In this international inspection process, are the citizens of the United States, including corporate citizens, protected from unreasonable searches and seizures?

Mr. MAHLEY. One of the explicit protections written into the convention at the U.S. insistence is that constitutional protections are indeed a reason for modifying the inspection procedure.

CONSTITUTIONALITY OF IMPLEMENTING LEGISLATION

Chairman HAMILTON. Can you give us a legal opinion concerning the constitutionality of the implementing legislation?

Mr. MAHLEY. Sir, I am not myself a lawyer, but my general counsel and the other general counsels of the executive branch agencies of the U.S. Government have concluded the implementing legislation is constitutional, yes, sir.

Chairman HAMILTON. Would you furnish us that opinion, please?

Mr. MAHLEY. Yes, sir.[3]

Chairman HAMILTON. Mr. Browder, do you have some questions?

IMPACT OF CONVENTION ON CHEMICAL WEAPONS DEFENSE CAPABILITIES

Mr. BROWDER. Yes, Mr. Chairman. I think the hearings so far have dealt very adequately with the need for this convention and implementing legislation, and with the questions, the very serious questions regarding our chemical industry.

I would like to ask you a couple of questions about what I consider some second tier concerns that we have. I would like to get a response from the panel.

One of the concerns—and I would like to ask Mr. Moodie and Mr. Mahley to respond to this concern—one of the concerns that some of us have in terms of our national defense—one of the concerns is that there will be an illusion that if we have the Chemical Weapons Convention, we have no more need for a strong chemical defense. Not only is that something that may be—maybe would be encouraged by what the Chemical Weapons Convention stands for, but it would be a practical concern for us in Congress as we debate future defense budgets.

Could you tell me whether you think that the Chemical Weapons Convention decreases, or what impact that will have on our ability to defend ourselves against people who did not sign or abide by the Chemical Weapons Convention?

---

[3] The information appears in the appendix.

Mr. MOODIE. I think that issue will evolve over time, sir. But certainly at the time of the convention's entry into force and the uncertainty as to who exactly will and will not be a party to that convention at that time, early in its stages, I don't think that there is any reason for the United States to diminish its attention to and funding of chemical defense programs. There could still be the rogue state like Saddam Hussein, who will continue to pursue a chemical capability which may at some point in the future be used against the United States and U.S. forces. They have to be adequately protected against that.

I tried to make a point in my testimony that the existence of the convention does not obviate the need for such a program. I think that one of the things—and this is not a criticism of the convention—that we have to be very sensitive to, is the sense of complacency that will lead us to diminish our efforts in other areas, which still requires time, attention and funding.

Mr. BROWDER. Mr. Mahley.

Mr. MAHLEY. Sir, I would say two things, one of them on behalf of the administration and the other as a personal statement.

On behalf of the administration, I will point out, we do not believe that the existence of the convention in any way detracts or otherwise reduces the continuing need for a vigorous and completely effective U.S. chemical defense capability, not only because of the rogue state question, but because we cannot by any means be absolutely guaranteed, with the idea that we would be able to catch every potential violator and therefore reduce or eliminate completely the potential threat to U.S. Armed Forces personnel the exposure to chemical weapons. As you well know, that is something we do not want to do.

In addition to which, I would add my personal comment, as Mr. Moodie commented earlier, in terms of the fact Saddam Hussein did not use his chemical capability in the Gulf War. It is my own personal view that one of the contributing reasons for that was the very clear indication that while it might have indeed changed the U.S. war aims, it certainly was not going to significantly detract from the ability of the U.S. Armed Forces and the coalition armed forces to soundly defeat the Iraqi Armed Forces in combat. That is because we had enough defensive capability so that essentially we reacted in terms of our preparedness as if he had been prepared to employ that chemical weapons capability. We operated in spite of that.

That is exactly the kind of thing we need to be able to do in the future, so we simply tell in advance any potential violator; and it is one of the things which incidentally will help enforce the convention.

ARTICLE X

Mr. BROWDER. I would like to pursue specifically, Article X. Would you discuss that for us? That is a different argument.

Mr. MAHLEY. The different argument in Article X is the assistance provision. There is a provision in the convention that says any member state, any state party to the convention that feels itself threatened by the potential use of chemical weapons—and I emphasize the word "potential" here; not "actual," after the fact use, but potential use—has the right to appeal to the other member states for assistance in defeating the threat of that use against it. Therefore, we have not only the requirement to maintain, obviously, the United States' capability, but we also have the potential in that, depending upon subscription by the United States to the voluntary program, of having to provide chemical defense capability to other states that may feel threatened by either rogue states or violators of the convention.

Mr. BROWDER. So in our discussions about whether or not we ratify the Chemical Weapons Convention, this is a serious consideration on our part as probably the foremost country in the world in t r s of chemical defense that we may be called on through Article X im——

Mr. MAHLEY. I think indeed—yes, sir. I think indeed there is a real probability the United States will be requested by states at some point in the future to provide assistance under Article X.

READINESS TO IMPLEMENT VERIFICATION REGIME

Mr. BROWDER. Let me ask what happens if we have ratification by the 65th state. Will inspectors and a verification regime be ready? I visited with you in The Hague with the Preparatory Commission, and that is an issue that has been raised. Will we be ready if we get 65 states to ratify this convention?

Mr. MAHLEY. I will give you my professional judgment on that, sir. It is yes.

While I cannot guarantee what the international organization is going to do—I know we prepared both the training programs, the budget, prepared the manpower levels—we have begun already selecting among the large number of applicants for the international organization—begun selecting among the large number of applicants for the positions of inspectors in terms of their qualifications and the like. We have already set in place and enforced the means of procuring the various pieces of equipment necessary to man the inspection sets when they are going to be ready.

I think at this point we can say, yes, sir, we will be ready to implement the convention once we get the 65 ratifications and 180 days ramp-up time.

Mr. BROWDER. Mr. Carpenter.

EDUCATING INDUSTRY ON NEW REGULATORY REGIME

Mr. CARPENTER. I would like to bring to your attention another aspect of being ready. If we strip away the terms of the treaty, this is really a new regulation for the chemical industry. This is going to be a fairly complicated regulation, and it is going to bring in industries that are not usually regulated to the extent that the regular chemical industry is.

Pull a number out of the air. When you have 8,000 sites, this is probably one of the more complicated regulations that we will have tried to initiate since the Toxic Substances Control Act. It takes a lot of effort and resources on both sides of that equation, the regulated and the regulators, to make that happen.

I think it is going to be a substantial task to bring industry up to speed about their obligations, and it will be necessary for the

Congress and for the national authority to make sure that appropriate resources are available to implement this.

Now I must say that ACDA has really made a substantial effort to educate industry and bring them up to speed. We have tried to be participants and assist them in doing that. Nevertheless, a great deal of those industries, companies, specific sites are not aware that they are about to have the pleasure of participating.

I think it is going to be awfully important that appropriate resources be made available to do this thing right the first time.

Mr. MOODIE. Sir, may I just reinforce that a little bit?

One of the objectives of the organization with which I am now involved is to educate and assist industry in meeting their obligations under the convention. In response to a recent mailing of some educational materials to a variety of industry representatives, the primary reaction we got was, why are you sending this to me; I don't make chemical weapons.

When we explained there are provisions under the treaty, declarations and so on, to which you may have to respond, all of a sudden the people at the other end of the phone became much more interested.

I think Mr. Carpenter's comments about heightening the awareness within industry of this issue is extremely important, in part because one of the things that we learned in doing those trial inspections, and that others have learned from the inspections that they have done, is that the best way to deal with the issue, the thing that is most important for a smooth and effective implementation is prior preparation. If industry is prepared, they are going to be much better able to handle this than if international inspectors show up at their door sometime, and they are surprised about it.

TRAINING OF INTERNATIONAL INSPECTORS

Mr. BROWDER. Mr. Chairman, I will close this.

If I may just have a minute to pursue this, it is not only for the people that have to live under this but our financial obligations as the U.S. Congress to this—to these inspections.

The question of educating the people that will have to live with it, but also the problem of perhaps inspectors engaging in industrial espionage.

Mr. Mahley, where does the training of international inspectors stand now?

Mr. MAHLEY. Right now, it stands in the fact that we have completed the training of what I will call the "first cadre" of those who have been hired by the Provisional Technical Secretariat in preparation for managing the Technical Secretariat. Those people are in place.

The actual inspector hire we have deferred and have not actually accomplished, until such time as we have gotten the 6-month ramp-up period. That is when we are going to actually bring the inspectors on board. We are saving money by not having them as employees of the international organization yet, which means what we are doing in the process of training at this point is that various nations, including the United States, are offering training programs for candidate inspectors.

Now, the thing that I want to emphasize in saying they are candidate inspectors is that we made very certain that there is no guarantee on the part of the international organization that because someone has completed a training program that means they are automatically going to be hired as one of the international inspectors. There are political and technical quotas that will be engaged in the hiring process. We want to make sure if somebody else offers a training program that may be inferior to what we think is needed, that that does not automatically give them a certificate that says, I am entitled to become an inspector.

Mr. BROWDER. You are satisfied you are making satisfactory progress?

Mr. MAHLEY. I am satisfied we have in place the training programs that will be able to provide first-rate training to those inspectors during that 6-month period, yes, sir.

U.S. CONTRIBUTION TO FUNDING OF PREPCOM

Mr. BROWDER. The PREPCOM, what is the U.S. share of funding for that? Are there any funding shortfalls projected?

Mr. MAHLEY. At the moment, sir, our projected funding for that, for the coming calendar year, 1995, is going to be roughly $12 million; now that is, given some assumptions about ramp-up.

In terms of this calendar year, we made a full contribution of the United States' amount and, as indicated, that as a matter of fact did not even require all of the money that the committee, as well as others, was able to appropriate for us in our budget for the current fiscal year.

I am sorry, I fudge a little bit between those. The PREPCOM does things on a calendar year basis while the United States does things on a fiscal year basis.

I would point out that one of the things that we are very proud of in what we have done in the Preparatory Commission work is that it has been largely due to U.S. insistence on doing things in a cost-effective fashion that trimmed the original draft budget submitted by the international organization for the current calendar year, trimmed our responsibility, the U.S. contribution, from some $14 million to $7.1 million.

As I say, I am dubious in terms of giving you a firm figure for calendar 1995 because that will depend upon when we start the ramp-up period.

Mr. BROWDER. That is something we have been involved with and will continue to be interested in.

Thank you, Mr. Chairman.

NUMBER OF COUNTRIES PRODUCING CHEMICAL WEAPONS

Chairman HAMILTON. How many countries are producing chemical weapons today?

Mr. MOODIE. Unofficial estimates in the open literature suggest in the neighborhood of two dozen pursuing a chemical weapons program. What this literature means by a "program," however, is often left undefined as to whether it is actual production, research, development, and where they are in the process.

Chairman HAMILTON. What are some of the countries?

Mr. MOODIE. North Korea, Libya, Syria, and Iraq; it depends upon the list you see. Some people will have question marks about countries where there seems to be less certainty, or that countries have had chemical weapons programs in the past but may no longer do so.

Chairman HAMILTON. The countries on that list, do you expect any of them to become members of the convention?

Mr. MAHLEY. The answer to that, sir, is yes.

Chairman HAMILTON. Which ones?

Mr. MAHLEY. Well, of the members of the—of the countries on the two dozen nation list, I expect some to become members of the convention. Of those that have been specifically named by Mr. Moodie, none of them is currently signatory to the convention.

Chairman HAMILTON. Which countries producing chemical weapons do you expect to become members of the convention?

Mr. MAHLEY. Well, sir, I would expect Iran to be in that category.

Chairman HAMILTON. Iran.

Mr. MAHLEY. Yes, sir.

Chairman HAMILTON. Any others?

Mr. MAHLEY. I don't think I prefer to go in this hearing beyond that statement.

Chairman HAMILTON. There are others, though?

Mr. MAHLEY. Yes, sir.

Chairman HAMILTON. Countries like Libya, Iraq, Iran, and North Korea—you said Iran might join, but the others will not join, presumably.

Mr. MAHLEY. At least not immediately. They are not currently signatories.

MAINTAINING CHEMICAL WEAPONS DETERRENT CAPABILITY

Chairman HAMILTON. How do you answer the complaint they can go ahead with the production of chemical weapons? We are restraining ourselves; other countries are restraining themselves.

Mr. MAHLEY. Well, I would answer that in a number of ways, sir.

Number one, as General Shalikashvili indicated to the Senate Foreign Relations Committee hearings on this same convention, the fact of other people producing chemical weapons does not mean the United States should or even desires to produce chemical weapons as a retaliatory capability. There are other means we have of deterring the use of chemical weapons against us.

The second thing I would refer you to is the fact, if we can establish this convention and therefore establish not only the norm but the provisions of this convention, which will put an enormous amount of pressure on those countries, first of all, to join the convention because it will become increasingly more difficult for them to get the wherewithal to do their chemical weapons production programs outside of the treaty regime, because a number of the crucial chemicals to such a program will be denied them in international commerce as nonparties to the convention.

Chairman HAMILTON. You don't see any jeopardy to the U.S. national interest if these countries can continue to produce chemical weapons and we do not?

Mr. MAHLEY. No, sir. I do not believe the United States intends to produce chemical weapons even without this treaty. So our forgoing of production of chemical weapons does not constitute a net debit to our national security.

Chairman HAMILTON. Thank you very much. We appreciate your participation.

The committee stands adjourned.

[Whereupon, at 11:30 a.m., the committee was adjourned.]

PREPARED STATEMENTS

Prepared Statement of Donald A. Mahley, Acting Assistant Director, Bureau of Multilateral Affairs, U.S. Arms Control and Disarmament Agency

The Chemical Weapons Convention (CWC) contains a number of provisions that require implementing legislation to give them effect within the United States. These include provisions on international inspections, declarations by the chemical industry, and the establishment of a "National Authority." In addition, the CWC specifically requires the U.S. Government to apply the prohibitions in the Convention to all individuals and legal entities (such as corporations) within the United States, regardless of nationality, and to all American citizens living outside the U.S. To meet these obligations, on May 27, 1994 the Administration submitted to the Congress the proposed "Chemical Weapons Convention Implementation Act of 1994."

During the development of the proposed Act, comments were solicited from industry, specifically the Chemical Manufacturers Association and twelve other industry associations, and from the staffs of the relevant Congressional committees. In addition, the draft incorporates as much legislative precedent as possible. The principal statutes used as models were the Biological Weapons Anti-Terrorism Act (for the criminal provisions) and the Toxic Substances Control Act (for provisions concerning declarations and inspections).

U.S. industry, while noting that a few areas need further work, has been favorably disposed toward the proposed Act. In particular, the Chemical Manufacturers Association (CMA) has stressed the importance to industry of the legislation's strong protections against disclosure of confidential business information, its declared policy of taking the competitive impact on industry into account during U.S. implementation of the CWC, and its provision for industry input into facility agreements governing inspections of chemical facilities.

OVERVIEW OF THE LEGISLATION

Before getting into the specifics of the proposed Act, it is useful to provide a general outline of its contents. The

proposed Act contains six miscellaneous sections and four
Titles. The six sections cover the short title of the Act, the
table of contents, Congressional findings and declarations,
definitions, and a severability clause. Title I provides the
authority for the President to establish the U.S. National
Authority. Title II contains criminal prohibitions with regard
to activities relating to chemical weapons (e.g., outlawing
their possession, development, and use) and criminal
prohibitions on the use of riot-control agents as a method of
warfare. This Title also implements the CWC's restrictions on
activities related to Schedule 1 and 2 chemicals, such as the
prohibition on transfers to non-Parties.

Title III contains provisions authorizing the U.S.
Government to collect information from members of the chemical
industry as required by the CWC. This Title also prohibits the
disclosure of information or materials (e.g., samples) obtained
under the CWC except to the Organization for the Prohibition of
Chemical Weapons (OPCW) and to CWC States Parties, to
appropriate committees of the Congress, for law-enforcement
purposes, or when disclosure is determined to be in the
national interest. Significant civil and criminal penalties
are provided for unauthorized disclosures. At the same time,
this Title outlaws the failure to provide such information or
materials, and provides penalties for those who refuse to do so.

Finally, Title IV sets forth procedures for the initiation
and conduct of the international inspections required by the
CWC. This Title includes provisions regarding notice and
credentials, scope and timeframes of inspections, sampling,
facility agreements, safety procedures, and U.S. Government
cooperation. It also contains legal mechanisms for ensuring
that the United States can fulfill its CWC obligation to allow
inspections, such as procedures for obtaining warrants.
Finally, Title IV prohibits the refusal to allow inspections,
as well as interference with them.

These, in brief, are the areas covered by the proposed
Act. The following discussion provides some additional details.

MISCELLANEOUS SECTIONS

The first part of the proposed Act consists of six
miscellaneous sections. In addition to standard sections such
as the short title of the Act, the first part contains
Congressional findings and declarations, and definitions.

The Congressional findings demonstrate that body's
recognition of the importance of the significant threat posed
by chemical weapons, the essential role of the CWC in
addressing this problem, and the significance of the
verification regime for the success of the Convention,
including the necessity of inspections and declarations. These

findings provide a clear legislative rationale for international inspections of facilities and locations within the entire United States, and will be important for any subsequent judicial review of the proposed Act.

There are also three Congressional declarations regarding U.S. policy with regard to the implementation of the CWC. The first two concern the provision of legal assistance to other States Parties to the CWC and ensuring the safety of people and protection of the environment during CWC implementation. At the suggestion of CMA, a third declaration on minimizing the burden of the Convention on the U.S. business community has been added. It reads as follows:

"It shall be the policy of the United States to minimize, to the greatest extent practicable, the administrative burden and intrusiveness of measures to implement the Chemical Weapons Convention placed on commercial and other private entities, and to take into account the possible competitive impact of regulatory measures on industry, consistent with the obligations of the United States under the Convention."

Finally, the definitions section incorporates the definitions set forth in the CWC, as well as definitions of additional terms used in the Act, such as "United States" and "person." The term "United States" reflects the CWC's understanding of the geographic scope of its obligations, i.e., all places under the jurisdiction or control of a State Party. Places under the jurisdiction or control of the United States include U.S. territory and certain additional locations, such as U.S. aircraft and vessels. The term "person" is defined as broadly as possible to ensure that all possible entities are covered by the provisions. Such entities include any individual, corporation, partnership, firm, association, trust, estate, or public or private institution; any state or political subdivision thereof or any political entity within a state; any foreign government or nation, or any agency, instrumentality, or political subdivision of any such government or nation; or any other entity located in the United States. The term "person" also includes any legal successor, representative, agent, or agency of the foregoing located in the United States.

TITLE I - NATIONAL AUTHORITY

Title I provides for the establishment of a National Authority to serve, among other things, as the national focal point for effective liaison between the United States and the OPCW and other States Parties to the Convention. The proposed Act requires the President to establish such a National Authority, but leaves it up to the Executive Branch to determine the appropriate structure.

TITLE II - APPLICATION OF CONVENTION PROHIBITIONS TO NATURAL
AND LEGAL PERSONS

Title II provides for criminal sanctions with regard to
activities relating to chemical weapons. It includes criminal
penalties, procedures for seizure, forfeiture and destruction
of chemical weapons, and provisions for injunctions on
prohibited activities. Violators can be fined or imprisoned
for life or any term of years, or both. This part of Title II
is modeled in large part on comparable language contained in
the Biological Weapons Anti-Terrorism Act. That Act implements
a similar obligation contained in the Biological Weapons
Convention. Title II also implements the CWC's restrictions on
activities related to Schedule 1 and 2 chemicals, such as the
prohibition on transfers to non-States Parties.

Title II is specifically required by paragraph 1 of
Article VII of the CWC, which obligates each State Party to
prohibit individuals and legal entities (such as corporations)
anywhere on its territory, or any other place under its
jurisdiction or control, from undertaking any activity
prohibited to the State Party itself under the Convention.
Article VII also requires each State Party to enact penal
legislation with respect to prohibited activities within its
borders and to such activities conducted by its citizens (but
not its businesses) outside its territory. In other words, if
you or your business engage in chemical weapons-related
activities within the United States, regardless of your
nationality or who owns your business, you are potentially
criminally liable for those activities. Moreover, if you are
an U.S. citizen, you can be held personally liable regardless
of where your activities take place.

It is important to note, at this point, that we are
talking about activities related to chemical weapons.
Specifically, Title II outlaws the knowing development,
production, other acquisition, stockpiling, retention, direct
or indirect transfer, use, ownership, or possession of any
chemical weapon. The assistance, encouragement, or inducement
of any person to do so, and attempt or conspiracy to do so, are
also prohibited. However, toxic chemicals are not considered
chemical weapons if they are intended for purposes not
prohibited under the CWC and if the types and quantities
present are consistent with such purposes. Peaceful purposes
for which toxic chemicals may be produced include industrial,
pharmaceutical, medical, agricultural, and research uses.
Thus, with certain restrictions, legitimate, peaceful uses of
toxic chemicals are not subject to criminal or other penalties.

In addition to banning chemical-weapons activities, the
CWC also bans certain otherwise permitted activities in
relation to the most dangerous chemicals, those listed on
Schedules 1 and 2. Title II tracks these restrictions in the
CWC by making it unlawful for any person to produce, acquire,

retain, transfer, or use Schedule 1 chemicals unless the following criteria are met. First, these chemicals must be used only for research, medical, pharmaceutical, or protective purposes. Second, the amounts used may not exceed limits to be established by the U.S. Government. Finally, the aggregate amount of Schedule 1 chemicals in the United States as a whole may not exceed one metric ton. Some of this quota will be used by the U.S. Government for protective purposes, such as determining the adequacy of chemical defensive equipment and measures. The proposed Act provides for the remainder of the quota to be apportioned among private individuals and legal entities doing permitted work with Schedule 1 chemicals.

In addition to these domestic constraints, the CWC contains restrictions on transfers of Schedule 1 and 2 chemicals to non-States Parties for nonproliferation reasons and as an incentive to join the Convention. Accordingly, Title II outlaws transfers of Schedule 1 chemicals to persons located in states not party to the Convention. Title II also prohibits transfers of Schedule 2 chemicals to any person located in a non-State Party, or receipts of such chemicals from any other person located in a non-State Party. Transfers through the territory of non-States Parties are allowed, as long as the end-user is located in a State Party. In accordance with the Convention, restrictions on transfers of Schedule 2 chemicals will not come into effect until three years after the CWC enters into force.

Finally, the effective date of Title II is the same as the date the CWC enters into force for the United States, to ensure that the prohibitions with regard to the U.S. Government and with regard to individuals and legal entities begin at the same time. The rest of the Act is intended to become effective prior to this date, so as to provide enough time to establish the required legal authority and procedures necessary to implement the Convention.

TITLE III - DECLARATIONS BY CHEMICAL INDUSTRY

Title III, which concerns declarations, and Title VI, which concerns inspections, are the key titles with respect to chemical industry. Title III contains provisions on reporting of information required by the CWC, restrictions on disclosure of information and materials obtained under the Convention, and penalties for failure to provide information or materials. A number of these provisions are modeled after similar provisions in the Toxic Substances Control Act, the closest analogue in U.S. domestic law to the verification regime created by the CWC.

Specifically, Title III requires affected members of the chemical industry to maintain, permit access to, and provide the information necessary for the United States to make the declarations required under the Convention. Failure to do so

is specifically prohibited, and civil and criminal penalties
are provided for violations. By the same token, Title III
requires the U.S. Government to avoid duplication of reporting
mandated by other laws by, inter alia, coordinating CWC
implementation among agencies and departments. The present
thinking within the Administration is that the Department of
Commerce will be responsible for collecting the necessary
information from industry, after which the ONA will collate and
assemble this information for transmittal to the OPCW. The
precise details of the information-collection process are still
being worked out. It is expected that these provisions will
not be contained in the implementing legislation but rather in
the subsequent regulations.

The Administration recognizes that the protection of
confidential information supplied by industry is one of the
keys to the successful implementation of the CWC. Accordingly,
in addition to the protections built into the Convention
itself, such as facility agreements and the provisions of the
Confidentiality Annex, the proposed Act contains strict
non-disclosure provisions. Specifically, the Act exempts
information and materials provided pursuant to declarations and
inspections from the provisions of the Freedom of Information
Act. If enacted, this provision will allow the U.S. Government
to protect all information or materials supplied by industry
without requiring an inquiry into whether there are proprietary
interests in such information or materials.

In addition, the proposed Act prohibits public release of
information obtained in CWC declarations and inspections except
for four types of disclosures: (1) to the OPCW and other States
Parties to the Convention; (2) to appropriate Congressional
committees and subcommittees; (3) to agencies and departments
for law-enforcement purposes; and (4) when disclosure is
determined to be in the national interest. Of particular note
is the exception for law-enforcement agencies. This exception
is designed primarily for the situation in which U.S.
Government personnel accompanying inspectors happen to witness
evidence of a crime. In this case, the Government would not be
precluded from using such information in any subsequent
prosecution, including one not directly related to enforcement
of the CWC.

Title III also provides for giving the supplier of
information or materials advance notice when the U.S.
Government intends to exercise the national-interest exception
and release CWC-related information or materials. This
provision is designed to give the affected persons an
opportunity to prepare for the disclosure of information or
materials in unusual cases that are not specifically provided
for in the other three exceptions to the general non-disclosure
requirement.

To add real teeth to these non-disclosure obligations, Title III also contains significant criminal penalties for the unauthorized, willful disclosure of information or materials obtained pursuant to the CWC. Offenders can be fined or sentenced to prison for up to five years. The nondisclosure provisions have also been made specifically applicable to members of the international inspection teams. While such individuals generally are immune from U.S. laws during their performance of official duties, they can be prosecuted when the Director-General of the Technical Secretariat waives their immunity.

TITLE IV - INSPECTIONS

Title IV contains procedures for conducting routine inspections of chemical industry by the OPCW Technical Secretariat, as well as other types of CWC inspections. This Title also contains legal mechanisms for compelling non-consentual inspections. To the extent possible consistent with U.S. obligations under the Convention, the proposed Act has been drafted in such a manner as to commit the U.S. Government to assist industry in protecting its rights during inspections. In addition, these provisions have been drafted so as to fully protect the Constitutional rights of individuals and legal entities. As with Title III, a number of these provisions are modeled after similar provisions in the Toxic Substances Control Act.

The first part of Title IV provides the domestic legal framework for the conduct of inspections of chemical industry by the international inspectors of the Technical Secretariat. Specifically, Title IV sets forth procedures with regard to authority to inspect, provision of notice and credentials, time-frames for inspections, scope of inspections, sampling and safety, facility agreements, and coordination among U.S. Government agencies and departments. While intended primarily for routine inspections of chemical industry, these procedures also apply to other types of inspections established by the Convention, e.g., challenge inspections of private facilities.

It is important to note that the procedures for international inspections involve U.S. Government participation and assistance. Title IV does not provide for separate inspections by the U.S. Government to enforce the CWC. Instead, for the purposes of U.S. law, the CWC will be enforced through existing U.S. law-enforcement mechanisms, although information gathered during international inspections may be used for this purpose.

The specifics of the enforcement procedures are as follows. First, Title IV requires the U.S. Government to provide notices of inspections and to present appropriate credentials for Technical Secretariat and U.S. Government personnel. At the suggestion of CMA, separate notices will be given to the owner of the facility and to the operator, occupant, or agent in charge of the facility, although separate notices are not required for each entry. Also, while a notice is required to conduct an inspection, failure to receive a notice cannot bar an inspection. The notice provided by the U.S. Government will contain all appropriate information supplied by the Technical Secretariat. The Government is not, however, required to provide information that is classified or otherwise sensitive.

Second, Title IV requires that, consistent with the provisions of the CWC, all inspections must begin and end with reasonable promptness and occur at reasonable times, within reasonable limits, and in a reasonable manner. In particular, the U.S. Government should endeavor to ensure that, to the extent possible consistent with the CWC, each inspection takes place during ordinary working hours.

Third, Title IV sets forth the permitted scope of inspections conducted pursuant to the CWC. In general, an inspection may extend to all things within the premises to be inspected that can be considered relevant to CWC compliance. However, to the extent possible consistent with the CWC, no inspection can extend to data on financial matters, sales and marketing (other than shipments), pricing, personnel, research, patents, or environmental and health regulations. In other words, those data considered most sensitive to proprietary concerns and least relevant to CWC compliance will be given the most protection. The United States cannot flatly prohibit collection of such information by the Technical Secretariat. Nevertheless, the U.S. Government will endeavor to ensure that, to the extent permitted by the CWC, information not relevant to compliance is protected from disclosure.

Fourth, Title IV provides for the conclusion of facility agreements for facilities subject to routine inspection. Facilities that have such agreements must be inspected in accordance with them. Facility agreements are mandatory for Schedule 1 facilities and are also required for Schedule 2 facilities, unless the Technical Secretariat and the inspected Party agree otherwise. Facility agreements are optional for Schedule 3 facilities and "other" chemical production facilities subject to routine inspection, but the proposed Act creates an expectation that the U.S. Government will conclude facility agreements for such facilities upon request. Finally, the proposed provisions of Title IV make it clear that facility owners and operators, occupants, or agents in charge should be involved in the negotiation of all required and requested facility agreements to the extent practicable, consistent with U.S. obligations under the CWC.

Fifth, Title IV requires CWC inspectors and accompanying U.S. Government personnel to observe the safety regulations of the inspected facility. This provision extends to U.S. Government personnel an identical obligation for CWC inspection teams contained in the Convention. Title IV also authorizes the U.S. Government to require the provision of samples as mandated by the CWC, but makes clear that the facilities have the final word as to who will take the samples.

Finally, Title IV requires the U.S. Government, to the extent consistent with the CWC, to assist inspected facilities in interacting with the inspection team.

These, then, constitute the measures the Administration will propose for protecting industry during the implementation of routine inspections. Implementation of the other types of inspections will follow the same procedures, as appropriate. The major difference will be that the agencies involved will differ, depending on the specific situation.

The U.S. Government expects that the vast majority of inspections will be conducted voluntarily. Accordingly, the provisions for inspections have been constructed on this basis. Nevertheless, because the United States must faithfully implement its obligation under the CWC to allow short-notice inspections of any site, declared or undeclared, the proposed Act also contains a number of legal mechanisms for compelling access where facilities refuse to provide it voluntarily. The basic legal cornerstone for ensuring this is the Title IV provision making unlawful the failure or refusal to permit entry, and the disruption, delay, or impediment of an inspection. Since the CWC specifically allows inspected facilities -- particularly during challenge inspections -- to take measures to protect confidential information that could, in effect, "disrupt, delay, or impede" an inspection, Title IV bans only those delaying actions not permitted by the CWC.

U.S. courts are empowered to enforce the access provision by restraining violations and compelling the taking of any action required by the Act or the CWC. Penalties for violations include fines and imprisonment for up to two years. Unlike violations of the reporting requirements, fines for this type of violation could be assessed on a daily basis, as a means of applying additional pressure on those who refuse access. To.balance these rather serious penalties, under the proposed Act the U.S. Government must provide notice and a hearing prior to assessment of a penalty, must take into account factors such as the circumstances of the violation and the violator's ability to pay, and may modify the penalty. In addition, Title IV provides for judicial review of the penalty.

Title IV also establishes procedures for obtaining search warrants, as well as subpoenas requiring the attendance and testimony of witnesses and the production of information. These procedures are designed to meet the Constitutional requirements for the issuance of warrants on the basis of "administrative probable cause," i.e., the standards for issuing warrants under administrative inspections rather than the standards used for criminal searches. The same procedures can also be used to obtain criminal search warrants, if needed.

Finally, Title IV prohibits courts from issuing injunctions or other orders limiting the ability of the Technical Secretariat to conduct inspections or the U.S. Government to facilitate them. One reason for this provision is that even if injunctions are later lifted, they could keep the U.S. from meeting the short deadlines for initiating inspections required by the CWC.

CONCLUSION

The Administration's proposed implementing legislation for the Chemical Weapons Convention provides the necessary elements for implementing the CWC. While the Administration is committed to continuing to work with industry, the Congress, and other affected parties in shaping this legislation, we believe our proposal is reasonable, balanced, and fair.

Prepared Statement of Dr. Will Carpenter on Behalf of the Chemical Manufacturers Association

Good morning Mr. Chairman. My name is Will Carpenter. I am Vice-Chairman of the Board of Agridyne Corporation, appearing today on behalf of the Chemical Manufacturers Association (CMA). I appreciate this opportunity to attest to the chemical industry's support for the legislation to implement the Chemical Weapons Convention (CWC).

My message to the Committee today is straightforward. CMA strongly supports the Chemical Weapons Convention. And we strongly support effective, efficient and practical measures to implement the Convention. Your hearing today is a means of assuring that we meet the challenge of complete CWC implementation.

Before I delve into the specifics, I want to make special mention of the commitment and leadership demonstrated by Martin Lancaster to the goal of eradicating chemical weapons. He is Congress' true expert on the CWC, and he has devoted a great deal of time and attention to making sure that the CWC is a good deal for the United States. He's tackled the thorny issues in chemical arms control; he's tackled the particular problem of the Russian CW stocks. The CWC is in no small part a result of his commitment.

We would not be here today without the hard work of Don Mahley and the negotiators at the U.S. Arms Control and Disarmament Agency. We would not be here today if you, Mr. Chairman, had not committed valuable resources in tracking the CWC. And from my point of view, we would not be here today were it not for my industry's conviction that chemical weapons can be eliminated. The CWC is, in our view, a verifiable convention.

Our conviction springs from a belief that with the chemical industry as a partner we could develop a new arms control mechanism that addressed both national security concerns and the needs of commercial interests. The CWC achieves those objectives. Our goal now is to assure that those principles are reflected in U.S. law.

One of our industry's goals in the ongoing implementation process is to assure that the CWC remains an arms control agreement. It was not conceived as a means of serving other policy goals, or as a means of expanding the regulatory reach over the commercial industry. CMA helped develop the CWC verification system at the multilateral level, and we need your Committee's attention to making sure that system is exactly what is delivered in the United States.

Make no mistake about it. The CWC will significantly impact the chemical industry. No other arms control agreement in history cuts so broadly and deeply into U.S. commerce. An unprecedented number of companies will be required to report their activities to the U.S. government. Commercial facilities will be required to open their doors to on-site inspections by an international agency, on a scale never before imagined.

The challenge is to get it right the first time. Let's not repeat the regulatory mistakes we've witnessed in so many other areas. There are inherent complexities in the CWC regulatory regime, and both Congress and the Administration must assure that the Department of Commerce has the resources to do the job right.

The implementing legislation crafted by the Clinton Administration is a good step in the right direction. I'm pleased to say that the Administration involved the industry in drafting their proposal, and the bill addresses most of our concerns.

No other legislation - to my knowledge - expresses a need to consider regulatory burden to the degree the CWC legislation does. The potential impact of public disclosure of industry declarations under the CWC is recognized in the proposal. The significant protections for legitimate commercial interests contained in the CWC can be fairly translated into U.S. law through this legislation.

We can help get CWC implementation right the first time by addressing several specific concerns. Our recommendations - detailed in an annex to my testimony - are designed to fully implement the CWC at a minimum burden to commercial interests.

The Administration took pains to mirror the CWC in drafting this legislation. The definitions contained in the legislation should not be generalized in a manner which broaden coverage of chemicals beyond that intended by the CWC.

The bill's penalty provisions should also be modified. Fines totaling $50,000 per day may be assessed for chemical weapons activities, and for violations of the reporting and inspection requirements. Applied to illegal weapons activities, there is a deterrent value in high potential penalties. But we question whether a penalty this high has any value in preventing minor reporting violations, or well-grounded refusals to permit an inspection. Furthermore, a per day penalty is more appropriate for situations where there is a high degree of culpability, and a great deal of resulting damage or harm. In the context of the CWC, this penalty provision will be difficult to apply. We strongly recommend that the Committee modify the penalty provisions of the proposal.

The CWC permits the host government to be present during international inspections. In general, CMA believes that U.S. representatives can act as intermediaries between the inspected facility and the inspection team. The legislation should make clear the intention that the representatives are members of either the lead agency or the national authority. CMA recommends that the extent to which U.S. representatives participate in inspection be limited.

The legislation does not express a commitment to adopt the Preparatory Commission's regulatory decisions as part of the U.S. regulatory regime. These regulatory decisions include matters such as declaration formats, inspection procedures, and possible exemptions for certain commercial activities, such as polymers and hydrocarbon facilities. If we are to meet the policy goal suggested in the legislation of reducing the burden and competitive impact of the CWC, the U.S. regulatory system must be no more burdensome than that implemented by other Parties to the Convention. CMA recommends that the Department of Commerce be charged with conforming the domestic regulatory system to that adopted by the Parties in the Hague. Regular reports to Congress from the Department of Commerce would provide an opportunity to monitor the competitive implications and burden of the CWC regulatory system.

Mr. Chairman, thank you again for the opportunity to testify today. As always, we are prepared to make available whatever assistance we can to you or your staff as this historic legislation is considered.

I would be happy to answer any questions the Committee might have.

CHEMICAL MANUFACTURERS ASSOCIATION

ANALYSIS OF AND RECOMMENDATIONS FOR THE
CHEMICAL WEAPONS CONVENTION IMPLEMENTATION ACT

The Chemical Manufacturers Association (CMA) has conducted a thorough analysis of the Administration's proposal to implement the Chemical Weapons Convention (CWC) (S. 2221 and H.R. 4849). The recommendations and suggestions which follow will assure full implementation of the CWC, while minimizing the potential burden and intrusiveness of the Convention on the commercial chemical industry.

CMA's comments are arranged on a section-by-section basis for ease of reference.

SECTION 1. Short Title. No Comment.

SECTION 2. Table of Contents. No Comment.

SECTION 3. Congressional Findings. No Comment.

SECTION 4. Congressional Declarations.

A. Section 4(3) contains a Congressional declaration that U.S. policy shall be to minimize the potential administrative burden and intrusiveness of CWC implementation on the commercial chemical industry, and to require that competitive impact be taken into account in implementing the Convention. CMA recommends that Congress consider establishing a requirement for regular reports on the competitive impact of the CWC.

B. Significant regulatory decisions about CWC implementation are already being made in the Hague, the site of the Preparatory Commission for the Organization for the Prohibition of Chemical Weapons. These regulatory decisions include matters such as declaration formats, inspection procedures, classification systems for confidential business information, and possible exemptions for certain commercial activities (such as polymer production and hydrocarbon facilities). In order to assure that the U.S. regulatory system is no more burdensome than that implemented by other countries party to the CWC, Section 4 (or possibly Sections 301 and 401, relating to reporting of information) should contain an express requirement to conform the domestic regulatory system to that adopted at the international level.

SECTION 5. Definitions. No Comment.

SECTION 6. Severability. No Comment.

TITLE I. National Authority. No Comment.

TITLE II. Application of Convention Prohibitions to Natural and Legal Persons.

SECTION 201. Criminal Provisions.

Several drafting modifications will also help clarify application of this provision. Any reference to "chemical weapon" should contain a cross-reference to the appropriate definition (Section 227D). The reference to "whoever" in Section 227(a) should be replaced by "any person who."

A. Section 201 amends the U.S. Criminal Code (by adding new Sections 227 through 227D to Title 18) to impose criminal penalties for activities related to "chemical weapons." The definitional portion of the section should not be interpreted to broaden coverage beyond the intend of the CWC. CMA recommends several modifications to Section 201 to clarify that it doesn't apply to generally regulate toxic chemicals.

B. Section 227(a) establishes the express prohibition on activities related to "chemical weapons." Because of the uncertainty created by the definition of "toxic chemical," CMA recommends that the term, as it is used throughout this Section, be modified to include the words "for purposes prohibited by the Treaty." This modification will help clarify that the mere possession of a "toxic chemical" is not to be considered possession of a chemical weapon, so long as the chemical is used for purposes not prohibited under the CWC. The industry's concern is that this definition could result in situations that allow prosecutors to make out a prima facie violation simply by showing the presence of a "toxic chemical."

C. Section 227A establishes the right of the U.S. to seize and destroy "chemical weapons." Although an affirmative defense is available under this provision, the provision as drafted has the potential to limit the use of this defense by legitimate commercial interests. The defense requires the accused organization to prove 1) that the "weapon" is for a purpose not prohibited under the Convention, and 2) that the "weapon" is of a type and quantity consistent with that purpose. The provision effectively reverses the burden of proof of a critical element of a charge, namely that the government should have to prove that a particular chemical use constitutes a violation of the Convention. In addition, the legislation does not further define the two criteria of the affirmative defense, which may cause significant practical problems in its use.

D. The definitions of "toxic chemical" and "precursors" contained in Section 227D should be identical with the definitions in the Convention. In both cases, the Convention includes the following language as part of the definition of these terms:

> For the purposes of implementing this Convention, [toxic chemicals] [precursors] which have been identified for the application of verification measures are listed in Schedules contained in the Annex on Chemicals. CWC, Art. II (2),(3).

E. CMA suggests that the term "State Party to the Convention" as used in Section 203 be further clarified to prevent confusion.

TITLE III. Declarations by Chemical Industry

SECTION 301. Reporting of Information. Section 301 authorizes the Department of Commerce to promulgate regulations for the declarations required under the CWC from the chemical industry. The provision requires that, "to the extent feasible," the National Authority shall not require any duplicative or unnecessary reports. As drafted, this provision is ambiguous at best. A more restrictive criteria than "feasibility" would require the Department of Commerce to take a hard look at what information is already provided to the U.S. government, thereby preventing the expensive, burdensome expansion of industry reporting requirements. In addition, the provisions on duplicative or unnecessary reports applies only to the National Authority (i.e., the Arms Control and Disarmament Agency, ACDA), and not the Department of Commerce. CMA recommends that the restriction be extended to regulations issued by the Department of Commerce as well.

SECTION 302. Disclosure of Information or Materials. Section 302 provides for the limited disclosure of materials provided to the U.S. government in compliance with CWC obligations. Reported information is to be disclosed as required under the CWC, to appropriate Congressional committees, for law enforcement purposes, and when it is considered "in the national interest."

CMA believes that Section 302 can be strengthened with a few simple modifications. First, the provision should contain an express reference to the 5 U.S.C. § 552(b)(3), the Freedom of Information Act exemption upon which this provision was drafted. Further, the circumstances under which disclosures are permitted should be limited to "only those permitted under this Section." Disclosures made to law enforcement officials should be based on reasonable cause to believe that a crime has been committed. Finally, the term "national interest" as it is used in this Section should be more carefully defined to prevent inappropriate disclosures of confidential information, or use of the information for purposes other than CWC compliance.

TITLE IV. Inspections.

SECTION 401. Inspections of Chemical Industry.

A. Section 401 provides the authority for members of international inspection teams to enter chemical facilities for inspections under the CWC. The provision also authorizes representatives of **any** U.S. department or agency to accompany the team. Throughout the negotiations, the chemical industry advocated inspection procedures that would allow a minimum number of inspectors to quickly and efficiently conduct routine inspections, with little or no disruption.

CMA believes that the implementing legislation should adopt a limit on the number and extent to which U.S. representatives participate in on-site inspections. In general, CMA welcomes the availability of a U.S. government representative to act as an intermediary between the inspected facility and the inspection team. That intermediary function can be performed well from a central-location, such as the administrative facility assigned for the inspection team's use. It should be understood that the U.S. representatives are to be members of the lead agency or national authority. More extensive participation in an inspection should only be permitted at the request of the inspection facility. CMA is particularly concerned that appropriate limits are necessary for the participation of U.S. representatives due to safety and liability considerations.

Under Section 401, facilities are also required to receive notice of an impending inspection as soon as possible. CMA recommends that the National Authority consider appropriate alternatives for assuring adequate notice to the facility. Such alternatives include notice to both the site and to the corporate headquarters, and the use of electronic communications, such as telefax notice.

SECTION 402. No comment.

SECTION 403. No comment.

SECTION 404. Penalties. Section 404 contains the civil and criminal penalties applicable to violations of the provisions on weapons (Sec. 203), reporting (Sec. 303), and inspections (Sec. 404).

A. A $50,000 per day penalty is to be assessed for violations of the reporting and inspection requirements of the implementing legislation. CMA is particularly concerned that this penalty may be applied to even the most minor reporting violations. Due to incomplete knowledge of the CWC in potentially affected facilities, there may be less than complete compliance with the reporting requirements in the initial stages of implementation. Inadvertent reporting violations -- which will be essentially unintentional mistakes or accidents -- should not be subject to a $50,000 per day penalty.

CMA also believes that the $50,000 figure is excessive, compared to the harm likely to result from either a reporting violation or a failure to permit an inspection. Moreover, CMA objects to the use of a per-day penalty provision as an incentive for permitting inspections. Per-day penalties at such a high level are more appropriate in situations where the defendant has a high degree of culpability and there is a great deal of resulting damage.

The penalty provision may well be difficult to apply in practice. Assume, for example, that an inspection team arrives at a facility and are refused entry. Later that day, the inspection team leaves, and does not return (having moved on to other inspections) for a period of two to three months. Does the penalty provision apply to the entire period prior to the inspection team's return? Although Section 404 requires that several factors be taken into account in setting the amount of the penalty, and expressly permits the Lead Agency (presumably the Department of Commerce in the case of a commercial facility) to modify or compromise a penalty claim, these provisions are not enough. In any alleged violation of Section 404, it may be unrealistic to expect that the government would be willing to compromise the penalty, particularly given the media coverage likely to accompany such an event.

B. Section 404 also contains a criminal penalty for knowing violations of Section 203, 303, and 403. In order to avoid the problems that have arisen in the enforcement of statutes containing similar "knowing" violation provisions, CMA recommends a number of modifications. Section 404 should be clarified to indicate that the term "knowing" means knowledge that an act is illegal, not simply the knowledge of the activity itself. Further, because of the possibility that the knowledge of an employee can be attributed to others in an organization, CMA suggests that the following language -- similar to that which appears in several environmental statutes -- be considered:

> In determining whether a defendant knew that the conduct constituted a violation, the person is responsible only for actual awareness or actual belief that he possessed, and knowledge possessed by a person other than the defendant but not by the defendant himself may not be attributed to the defendant.

SECTION 405. No comments.

SECTION 406. Legal Proceedings. Section 406 authorizes the issuance of administrative warrants as the basis for inspections at chemical facilities. Although the provision allows the warrant to be sought "from any official authorized to issue search warrants." CMA strongly recommends that the term "any official" be clarified to mean the appropriate official of the Lead Agency or National Authority. In light of the fact that the relevant agencies for CWC implementation do not now have an administrative warrant process, the use of a judicial warrant process may in fact be more efficient.

OTHER COMMENTS

Several other matters are not expressly covered in the implementing legislation. CMA suggests that addressing these matters will improve the administration of the CWC in the United States.

A. Effective Date. The provisions on industry declarations and inspections will come into effect on the date the legislation is enacted. Assuming that the CWC is not yet in force for the United States, the legislation could be read to give the Department of Commerce authority to require reports from, and inspect, chemical facilities. Since the CWC will not come into force for the United States until six months after the deposit of the 65th instrument of ratification, CMA recommends that Titles III and IV become effective only upon the later of 1) the deposit of the U.S. instrument of ratification, or 2) the date of enactment if after deposit.

B. Application to Export Control Laws. Certain inspections of chemical facilities involve the potential for technology transfers to foreign citizens that, under any other circumstance, would require a license from the Department of Commerce. CMA recommends that the legislation clarify that the provisions of the Export Administration Act or the Enhanced Proliferation Control Initiative do not apply to disclosures of information to international inspectors.

C. CMA further suggests that the Bureau of Export Administration (Commerce) and the Defense Trade Center (Department of State) be required to amend their regulations to conform to the CWC implementing legislation, and to coordinate their regulations with those issued pursuant to the CWC.

APPENDIX 1

103D CONGRESS
2D SESSION

H. R. 4849

To implement the obligations of the United States under the Convention on the Prohibition of the Development, Production, Stockpiling and Use of Chemical Weapons and on Their Destruction, known as the "Chemical Weapons Convention" and opened for signature and signed by the United States on January 13, 1993.

IN THE HOUSE OF REPRESENTATIVES

JULY 28, 1994

Mr. HAMILTON (by request)(for himself, Mr. GILMAN, Mr. LANTOS, Mr. BERMAN, Mr. SWIFT, and Mr. OXLEY) introduced the following bill; which was referred jointly to the Committees on Foreign Affairs, the Judiciary, and Energy and Commerce

---

A BILL

To implement the obligations of the United States under the Convention on the Prohibition of the Development, Production, Stockpiling and Use of Chemical Weapons and on Their Destruction, known as the "Chemical Weapons Convention" and opened for signature and signed by the United States on January 13, 1993.

Be it enacted by the Senate and House of Representa-

2 *tives of the United States of America in Congress assembled,*

3 **SECTION 1. SHORT TITLE.**

4   This Act may be cited as the "Chemical Weapons

5 Convention Implementation Act of 1994".

(53)

1 **SEC. 2. TABLE OF CONTENTS.**

2   The table of contents for this Act is as follows—

3 **SEC. 3. CONGRESSIONAL FINDINGS.**

4   The Congress makes the following findings:

5   (1) Chemical weapons pose a significant threat

6 to the national security of the United States and are

7 a scourge to humankind.

8   (2) The Chemical Weapons Convention is the

9 best means of ensuring the nonproliferation of chem-

10 ical weapons and their eventual destruction and for-

11 swearing by all nations.

(3) The verification procedures contained in the
2   Chemical Weapons Convention and the faithful ad-
3   herence of nations to them, including the United
4   States, are crucial to the success of the Convention.

5   (4) The declarations and inspections required
6   by the Chemical Weapons Convention are essential
7   for the effectiveness of the verification regime.

8   **SEC. 4. CONGRESSIONAL DECLARATIONS.**

9   The Congress makes the following declarations:

10   (1) It shall be the policy of the United States
11   to cooperate with other States parties to the Chemi-
12   cal Weapons Convention and afford the appropriate
13   form of legal assistance to facilitate the implementa-
14   tion of the prohibitions contained in title II of this
15   Act.

16   (2) It shall be the policy of the United States,
17   during the implementation of its obligations under
18   the Chemical Weapons Convention, to assign the
19   highest priority to ensuring the safety of people and
20   to protecting the environment, and to cooperate as
21   appropriate with other States parties to the Conven-
22   tion in this regard.

23   (3) It shall be the policy of the United States
24   to minimize, to the greatest extent practicable, the
25   administrative burden and intrusiveness of measures

to implement the Chemical Weapons Convention

2 placed on commercial and other private entities, and

3 to take into account the possible competitive impact

4 of regulatory measures on industry, consistent with

5 the obligations of the United States under the Con-

6 vention.

7 **SEC. 5. DEFINITIONS.**

8 (a) IN GENERAL.—Except as otherwise provided in

9 this Act, the definitions of the terms used in this Act shall

10 be those contained in the Chemical Weapons Convention.

11 (b) OTHER DEFINITIONS.—(1) The term "Chemical

12 Weapons Convention" means the Convention on the Prohi-

13 bition of the Development, Production, Stockpiling and

14 Use of Chemical Weapons and on Their Destruction,

15 opened for signature on January 13, 1993.

16 (2) The term "national of the United States" has the

17 same meaning given such term in section 101(a)(22) of

18 the Immigration and Nationality Act (8 U.S.C.

19 1101(a)(22)).

20 (3) The term "United States", when used in a geo-

21 graphical sense, includes all places under the jurisdiction

22 or control of the United States, including—

23 (A) any of the places within the provisions of

24 section 101(41) of the Federal Aviation Act of 1958,

25 as amended (49 U.S.C. App. Sec. 1301(41)),

(B) any public aircraft or civil aircraft of the
United States, as such terms are defined in sections
101 (36) and (18) of the Federal Aviation Act of
1958, as amended (49 U.S.C. App. Secs. 1301(36)
and 1301(18)), and

(C) any vessel of the United States, as such
term is defined in section 3(b) of the Maritime Drug
Enforcement Act, as amended (46 U.S.C. App. Sec.
1903(b)).

(4) The term "person", except as used in section 201
of this Act and as set forth below, means—

(A) any individual, corporation, partnership,
firm, association, trust, estate, public or private institution, any State or any political subdivision
thereof, or any political entity within a State, any
foreign government or nation or any agency, instrumentality or political subdivision of any such government or nation, or other entity located in the United
States; and

(B) any legal successor, representative, agent or
agency of the foregoing located in the United States.
The phrase "located in the United States" in the term
"person" shall not apply to the term "person" as used
in the phrase "person located outside the territory" in sec-

1 tions 203(b), 203(c), and 302(c) of this Act and "person

2 located in the territory" in section 203(b) of this Act.

3 (5) The term "Technical Secretariat" means the

4 Technical Secretariat of the Organization for the Prohibi-

5 tion of Chemical Weapons established by the Chemical

6 Weapons Convention.

7 **SEC. 6. SEVERABILITY.**

8 If any provision of this Act, or the application of such

9 provision to any person or circumstance, is held invalid,

10 the remainder of this Act, or the application of such provi-

11 sion to persons or circumstances other than those as to

12 which it is held invalid, shall not be affected thereby.

13 TITLE I—NATIONAL AUTHORITY

14 **SEC. 101. ESTABLISHMENT.**

15 Pursuant to paragraph 4 of Article VII of the Chemi-

16 cal Weapons Convention, the President or the designee of

17 the President shall establish the "United States National

18 Authority" to, inter alia, serve as the national focal point

19 for effective liaison with the Organization for the Prohibi-

20 tion of Chemical Weapons and other States Parties to the

21 Convention.

TITLE II—APPLICATION OF CONVENTION PROHIBITIONS TO NATURAL AND LEGAL PERSONS

SEC. 201. CRIMINAL PROVISIONS.

(a) IN GENERAL.—Part I of title 18, United States Code, is amended by—

(1) redesignating chapter 11A relating to child support as chapter 11B; and

(2) inserting after chapter 11 relating to bribery, graft and conflicts of interest the following new chapter:

"CHAPTER 11A—CHEMICAL WEAPONS

"Sec.
"227. Penalties and prohibitions with respect to chemical weapons.
"227A. Seizure, forfeiture, and destruction.
"227B. Injunctions.
"227C. Other prohibitions.
"227D. Definitions.

"SEC. 227. PENALTIES AND PROHIBITIONS WITH RESPECT TO CHEMICAL WEAPONS.

"(a) IN GENERAL.—Except as provided in subsection (b), whoever knowingly develops, produces, otherwise acquires, stockpiles, retains, directly or indirectly transfers, uses, owns or possesses any chemical weapon, or knowingly assists, encourages or induces, in any way, any person to do so, or attempts or conspires to do so, shall be

1 fined under this title or imprisoned for life or any term
2 of years, or both.

3   "(b) EXCLUSION.—Subsection (a) shall not apply to
4 the retention, ownership or possession of a chemical weap-
5 on, that is permitted by the Chemical Weapons Convention
6 pending the weapon's destruction, by any agency or de-
7 partment of the United States. This exclusion shall apply
8 to any person, including members of the Armed Forces
9 of the United States, who is authorized by any agency or
10 department of the United States to retain, own or possess
11 a chemical weapon, unless that person knows or should
12 have known that such retention, ownership or possession
13 is not permitted by the Chemical Weapons Convention.

14   "(c) JURISDICTION.—There is jurisdiction by the
15 United States over the prohibited activity in subsection (a)
16 if—

17   "(1) the prohibited activity takes place in the
18   United States, or

19   "(2) the prohibited activity takes place outside
20   of the United States and is committed by a national
21   of the United States.

22   "(d) ADDITIONAL PENALTY.—The court shall order
23 that any person convicted of any offense under this section
24 pay to the United States any expenses incurred incident
25 to the seizure, storage, handling, transportation and de-

1 struction or other disposition of property seized for the
2 violation of this section.

3 **"SEC. 227A. SEIZURE, FORFEITURE, AND DESTRUCTION.**

4   "(a) SEIZURE.—(1) Except as provided in paragraph
5 (2), the Attorney General may request the issuance, in the
6 same manner as provided for a search warrant, of a war-
7 rant authorizing the seizure of any chemical weapon de-
8 fined in section 227D(2)(A) of this title that is of a type
9 or quantity that under the circumstances is inconsistent
10 with the purposes not prohibited under the Chemical
11 Weapons Convention.

12   "(2) In exigent circumstances, seizure and destruc-
13 tion of any such chemical weapon described in paragraph
14 (a)(1) may be made by the Attorney General upon prob-
15 able cause without the necessity for a warrant.

16   "(b) PROCEDURE FOR FORFEITURE AND DESTRUC-
17 TION.—Property seized pursuant to subsection (a) shall
18 be forfeited to the United States. Except as inconsistent
19 herewith, the provisions of chapter 46 of this title relating
20 to civil forfeitures shall extend to a seizure or forfeiture
21 under this section. The Attorney General shall provide for
22 the destruction or other appropriate disposition of any
23 chemical weapon seized and forfeited pursuant to this sec-
24 tion.

"(c) AFFIRMATIVE DEFENSE.—It is an affirmative

2 defense against a forfeiture under subsection (b) that—

3   "(1) such alleged chemical weapon is for a pur-

4   pose not prohibited under the Chemical Weapons

5   Convention; and

6   "(2) such alleged chemical weapon is of a type

7   and quantity that under the circumstances is con-

8   sistent with that purpose.

9   "(d) OTHER SEIZURE, FORFEITURE, AND DESTRUC-

10 TION.—

11   "(1) Except as provided in paragraph (2), the

12   Attorney General may request the issuance, in the

13   same manner as provided for a search warrant, of

14   a warrant authorizing the seizure of any chemical

15   weapon defined in section 227D(2) (B) or (C) of

16   this title that exists by reason of conduct prohibited

17   under section 227 of this title.

18   "(2) In exigent circumstances, seizure and de-

19   struction of any such chemical weapon described in

20   paragraph (1) may be made by the Attorney General

21   upon probable cause without the necessity for a war-

22   rant.

23   "(3) Property seized pursuant to this sub-

24   section shall be summarily forfeited to the United

25   States and destroyed.

"(e) ASSISTANCE.—The Attorney General may re-
2 quest assistance from any agency or department in the
3 handling, storage, transportation or destruction of prop-
4 erty seized under this section.

5 "(f) OWNER LIABILITY.—The owner or possessor of
6 any property seized under this section shall be liable to
7 the United States for any expenses incurred incident to
8 the seizure, including any expenses relating to the han-
9 dling, storage, transportation and destruction or other dis-
10 position of the seized property.

11 **"SEC. 227B. INJUNCTIONS.**

12 "(a) IN GENERAL.—The United States may obtain
13 in a civil action an injunction against—

14   "(1) the conduct prohibited under section 227
15   of this title;

16   "(2) the preparation or solicitation to engage in
17   conduct prohibited under section 227 of this title; or

18   "(3) the development, production, other acquisi-
19   tion, stockpiling, retention, direct or indirect trans-
20   fer, use, ownership or possession, or the attempted
21   development, production, other acquisition, stock-
22   piling, retention, direct or indirect transfer, use,
23   ownership or possession, of any alleged chemical
24   weapon defined in section 227D(2)(A) of this title
25   that is of a type or quantity that under the cir-

cumstances is inconsistent with the purposes not

2 prohibited under the Chemical Weapons Convention,

3 or the assistance to any person to do so.

4 "(b) AFFIRMATIVE DEFENSE.—It is an affirmative

5 defense against an injunction under subsection (a)(3)

6 that—

7 "(1) the conduct sought to be enjoined is for a

8 purpose not prohibited under the Chemical Weapons

9 Convention; and

10 "(2) such alleged chemical weapon is of a type

11 and quantity that under the circumstances is con-

12 sistent with that purpose.

13 **"SEC. 227C. OTHER PROHIBITIONS.**

14 "(a) IN GENERAL.—Except as provided in subsection

15 (b), whoever knowingly uses riot control agents as a meth-

16 od of warfare, or knowingly assists any person to do so,

17 shall be fined under this title or imprisoned for a term

18 of not more than ten years, or both.

19 "(b) EXCLUSION.—Subsection (a) shall not apply to

20 members of the Armed Forces of the United States. Mem-

21 bers of the Armed Forces of the United States who use

22 riot control agents as a method of warfare shall be subject

23 to appropriate military penalties.

"(c) JURISDICTION.—There is jurisdiction by the

2 United States over the prohibited activity in subsection (a)

3 if—

4   "(1) the prohibited activity takes place in the

5   United States, or

6   "(2) the prohibited activity takes place outside

7   of the United States and is committed by a national

8   of the United States.

9 **"SEC. 227D. DEFINITIONS.**

10   "As used in this chapter, the term—

11   "(1) 'Chemical Weapons Convention' means the

12   Convention on the Prohibition of the Development,

13   Production, Stockpiling and Use of Chemical Weap-

14   ons and on Their Destruction, opened for signature

15   on January 13, 1993;

16   "(2) 'chemical weapon' means the following, to-

17   gether or separately:

18   "(A) a toxic chemical and its precursors,

19   except where intended for a purpose not prohib-

20   ited under the Chemical Weapons Convention,

21   as long as the type and quantity is consistent

22   with such a purpose;

23   "(B) a munition or device, specifically de-

24   signed to cause death or other harm through

25   the toxic properties of those toxic chemicals

specified in subparagraph (A), which would be released as a result of the employment of such munition or device; or

"(C) any equipment specifically designed for use directly in connection with the employment of munitions or devices specified in subparagraph (B);

"(3) 'toxic chemical' means any chemical which through its chemical action on life processes can cause death, temporary incapacitation or permanent harm to humans or animals. This includes all such chemicals, regardless of their origin or of their method of production, and regardless of whether they are produced in facilities, in munitions or elsewhere;

"(4) 'precursor' means any chemical reactant which takes part at any stage in the production by whatever method of a toxic chemical. This includes any key component of a binary or multicomponent chemical system;

"(5) 'key component of a binary or multicomponent chemical system' means the precursor which plays the most important role in determining the toxic properties of the final product and reacts rapidly with other chemicals in the binary or multicomponent system;

"(6) 'purpose not prohibited under the Chemi-
2 cal Weapons Convention' means—

3   "(A) industrial, agricultural, research,
4   medical, pharmaceutical or other peaceful pur-
5   poses;

6   "(B) protective purposes, namely those
7   purposes directly related to protection against
8   toxic chemicals and to protection against chemi-
9   cal weapons;

10   "(C) military purposes not connected with
11   the use of chemical weapons and not dependent
12   on the use of the toxic properties of chemicals
13   as a method of warfare; or

14   "(D) law enforcement purposes, including
15   domestic riot control purposes;

16   "(7) 'national of the United States' has the
17 same meaning given such term in section 101(a)(22)
18 of the Immigration and Nationality Act (8 U.S.C.
19 1101(a)(22));

20   "(8) 'United States,' when used in a geographi-
21 cal sense, includes all places under the jurisdiction
22 or control of the United States, including—

23   "(A) any of the places within the provi-
24   sions of section 101(41) of the Federal Aviation

Act of 1958, as amended (49 U.S.C. App. Sec.
1301(41)),

"(B) any public aircraft or civil aircraft of
the United States, as such terms are defined in
sections 101 (36) and (18) of the Federal Aviation Act of 1958, as amended (49 U.S.C. App.
Secs. 1301(36) and 1301(18)), and

"(C) any vessel of the United States, as
such term is defined in section 3(b) of the Maritime Drug Enforcement Act, as amended (46
U.S.C. App. Sec. 1903(b));

"(9) 'person' means—

"(A) any individual, corporation, partnership, firm, association, trust, estate, public or
private institution, any State or any political
subdivision thereof, or any political entity within a State, any foreign government or nation or
any agency, instrumentality or political subdivision of any such government or nation, or other
entity; and

"(B) any legal successor, representative,
agent or agency of the foregoing; and

"(10) 'riot control agent' means any chemical
not listed in a Schedule in the Annex on Chemicals
of the Chemical Weapons Convention, which can

produce rapidly in humans sensory irritation or dis-

2   abling physical effects which disappear within a

3   short time following termination of exposure."

4   (b) CLERICAL AMENDMENTS.—The table of chapters

5 for part I of title 18, United States Code, is amended by—

6   (1) in the item for chapter 11A relating to child

7   support, redesignating "11A" as "11B"; and

8   (2) inserting after the item for chapter 11 the

9   following new item:

"11A. CHEMICAL WEAPONS .... 227."

10 SEC. 202. EFFECTIVE DATE.

11   This title shall take effect on the date the Chemical

12 Weapons Convention enters into force for the United

13 States.

14 SEC. 203. RESTRICTIONS ON SCHEDULED CHEMICALS.

15   (a) SCHEDULE 1 ACTIVITIES.—It shall be unlawful

16 for any person or any national of the United States lo-

17 cated outside the United States to produce, acquire, re-

18 tain, transfer or use a chemical listed on Schedule 1 of

19 the Annex on Chemicals of the Chemical Weapons Conven-

20 tion, unless—

21   (1) the chemicals are applied to research, medi-

22   cal, pharmaceutical or protective purposes;

23   (2) the types and quantities of chemicals are

24   strictly limited to those that can be justified for such

25   purposes; and

(3) the amount of such chemicals per person at

2 any given time for such purposes does not exceed a

3 limit to be determined by the United States National

4 Authority, but in any case, does not exceed one met-

5 ric ton.

6 (b) EXTRATERRITORIAL ACTS.—(1) It shall be un-

7 lawful for any person or any national of the United States

8 located outside the United States to produce, acquire, re-

9 tain or use a chemical listed on Schedule 1 of the Annex

10 on Chemicals of the Chemical Weapons Convention out-

11 side the territories of the States Parties to the Convention

12 or to transfer such chemicals to any person located outside

13 the territory of the United States, except as provided for

14 in the Convention for transfer to a person located in the

15 territory of another State Party to the Convention.

16 (2) Beginning three years after the entry into force

17 of the Chemical Weapons Convention, it shall be unlawful

18 for any person or any national of the United States lo-

19 cated outside the United States to transfer a chemical list-

20 ed on Schedule 2 of the Annex on Chemicals of the Con-

21 vention to any person located outside the territory of a

22 State Party to the Convention or to receive such a chemi-

23 cal from any person located outside the territory of a State

24 Party to the Convention.

(c) JURISDICTION.—There is jurisdiction by the
2 United States over the prohibited activity in subsections
3 (a) and (b) if—

4   (1) the prohibited activity takes place in the
5   United States, or

6   (2) the prohibited activity takes place outside of
7   the United States and is committed by a national of
8   the United States.

TITLE III—DECLARATIONS BY CHEMICAL INDUSTRY

11 **SEC. 301. REPORTING OF INFORMATION.**

12   (a) REPORTS.—The Department of Commerce shall
13 promulgate regulations under which each person who pro-
14 duces, processes, consumes, exports or imports, or pro-
15 poses to produce, process, consume, export or import, a
16 chemical substance subject to the Chemical Weapons Con-
17 vention shall maintain and permit access to such records
18 and shall submit to the Department of Commerce such
19 reports as the United States National Authority may rea-
20 sonably require pursuant to the Chemical Weapons Con-
21 vention. The Department of Commerce shall promulgate
22 regulations pursuant to this title expeditiously, and may
23 amend or change such regulations as necessary.

24   (b) COORDINATION.—To the extent feasible, the
25 United States National Authority shall not require any re-

1 porting that is unnecessary, or duplicative of reporting re-
2 quired under any other Act. Agencies and departments
3 shall coordinate their actions with other agencies and de-
4 partments to avoid duplication of reporting by the affected
5 persons under this Act or any other Act.

6 **SEC. 302. DISCLOSURE OF INFORMATION OR MATERIALS.**

7   (a) IN GENERAL.—Any information or materials re-
8 ported to, or otherwise obtained by, the United States Na-
9 tional Authority or the Department of Commerce, or any
10 other agency or department under this Act or the Chemi-
11 cal Weapons Convention may be withheld from public dis-
12 closure or provision only to the extent permitted by law.
13 Information or materials obtained from declarations or in-
14 spections required by the Chemical Weapons Convention,
15 that are not already in the public domain, shall be with-
16 held from public disclosure or provision and shall not be
17 required to be disclosed pursuant to section 552 of title
18 5, United States Code, except that such information or
19 material—

20   (1) shall be disclosed or otherwise provided to
21   the Technical Secretariat or other States Parties to
22   the Chemical Weapons Convention in accordance
23   with the Convention, in particular, the provisions of
24   the Annex on the Protection of Confidential Infor-
25   mation;

(2) shall be made available to any committee or
subcommittee of Congress of appropriate jurisdiction
upon the written request of the chairman or ranking
minority member of such committee or subcommittee, except that no such committee or subcommittee,
or member thereof, shall disclose such information
or material;

(3) shall be disclosed to other agencies or departments for law enforcement purposes with regard
to this Act or any other Act, and may be disclosed
or otherwise provided when relevant in any proceeding under this Act or any other Act, except that disclosure or provision in such a proceeding shall be
made in such manner as to preserve confidentiality
to the extent practicable without impairing the proceeding; and

(4) may be disclosed, including in the form of
categories of information, if the United States National Authority determines that such disclosure is
in the national interest.

(b) NOTICE OF DISCLOSURE.—If the United States
National Authority, pursuant to subsection (a)(4), pro-
poses to publish or disclose or otherwise provide information or materials exempted from disclosure in subsection
(a), the United States National Authority shall, where ap-

1 propriate, notify the person who submitted such informa-

2 tion or materials of the intent to release such information

3 or materials. Where notice has been provided, the United

4 States National Authority may not release such informa-

5 tion or materials until the expiration of thirty days after

6 notice has been provided.

7   (c) CRIMINAL PENALTY FOR WRONGFUL DISCLO-

8 SURE.—Any officer or employee of the United States or

9 former officer or employee of the United States, who by

10 virtue of such employment or official position has obtained

11 possession of, or has access to, information or materials

12 the disclosure or other provision of which is prohibited by

13 subsection (a), and who knowing that disclosure or provi-

14 sion of such information or materials is prohibited by such

15 subsection, willfully discloses or otherwise provides the in-

16 formation or materials in any manner to any person, in-

17 cluding persons located outside the territory of the United

18 States, not entitled to receive it, shall be fined under title

19 18, United States Code, or imprisoned for not more than

20 five years, or both.

21   (d) INTERNATIONAL INSPECTORS.—The provisions of

22 this section on disclosure or provision of information or

23 materials shall also apply to employees of the Technical

24 Secretariat.

1 SEC. 303. PROHIBITED ACTS.

2   It shall be unlawful for any person to fail or refuse

3 to—

4   (a) establish or maintain records,

5   (b) submit reports, notices, or other information

6   to the Department of Commerce or the United

7   States National Authority, or

8   (c) permit access to or copying of records, as

9   required by this Act or a regulation thereunder.

TITLE IV—INSPECTIONS

11 SEC. 401. INSPECTIONS OF CHEMICAL INDUSTRY.

12   (a) AUTHORITY.—For purposes of administering this

13 Act—

14   (1) any duly designated member of an inspec-

15   tion team of the Technical Secretariat may inspect

16   any plant, plant site, or other facility or location in

17   the United States subject to inspection pursuant to

18   the Chemical Weapons Convention; and

19   (2) any duly designated representative of an

20   agency or department may accompany members of

21   an inspection team of the Technical Secretariat dur-

22   ing the inspection specified in paragraph (1).

23   (b) NOTICE.—An inspection pursuant to subsection

24 (a) may be made only upon issuance of a written notice

25 to the owner and to the operator, occupant or agent in

26 charge of the premises to be inspected, except that failure

1 to receive a notice shall not be a bar to the conduct of
2 an inspection. The notice shall be submitted to the owner
3 and to the operator, occupant or agent in charge as soon
4 as possible after the United States National Authority re-
5 ceives it from the Technical Secretariat. The notice shall
6 include all appropriate information supplied by the Tech-
7 nical Secretariat to the United States National Authority
8 regarding the basis for the selection of the plant site,
9 plant, or other facility or location for the type of inspection
10 sought, including, for challenge inspections pursuant to
11 Article IX of the Chemical Weapons Convention, appro-
12 priate evidence or reasons provided by the requesting
13 State Party to the Convention with regard to its concerns
14 about compliance with the Chemical Weapons Convention
15 at the facility or location. A separate notice shall be given
16 for each such inspection, but a notice shall not be required
17 for each entry made during the period covered by the in-
18 spection.

19   (c) CREDENTIALS.—If the owner, operator, occupant
20 or agent in charge of the premises to be inspected is
21 present, a member of the inspection team of the Technical
22 Secretariat, as well as, if present, the representatives of
23 agencies or departments, shall present appropriate creden-
24 tials before the inspection is commenced.

(d) TIME FRAME FOR INSPECTIONS.—Consistent

2 with the provisions of the Chemical Weapons Convention,

3 each inspection shall be commenced and completed with

4 reasonable promptness and shall be conducted at reason-

5 able times, within reasonable limits, and in a reasonable

6 manner. The Department of Commerce shall endeavor to

7 ensure that, to the extent possible, each inspection is com-

8 menced, conducted and concluded during ordinary work-

9 ing hours, but no inspection shall be prohibited or other-

10 wise disrupted for commencing, continuing or concluding

11 during other hours. However, nothing in this subsection

12 shall be interpreted as modifying the time frames estab-

13 lished in the Chemical Weapons Convention.

14   (e) SCOPE.—(1) Except as provided in paragraph (2)

15 of this subsection and subsection (f), an inspection con-

16 ducted under this title may extend to all things within the

17 premises inspected (including records, files, papers, proc-

18 esses, controls, structures and entering and exiting vehi-

19 cles) related to whether the requirements of the Chemical

20 Weapons Convention applicable to such premises have

21 been complied with.

22   (2) To the extent possible consistent with the obliga-

23 tions of the United States pursuant to the Chemical

24 Weapons Convention, no inspection under this title shall

25 extend to—

(A) financial data;

2 (B) sales and marketing data (other than ship-
3 ment data);

4 (C) pricing data;

5 (D) personnel data;

6 (E) research data;

7 (F) patent data; or

8 (G) data maintained for compliance with envi-
9 ronmental or occupational health and safety regula-
10 tions.

11 (f) FACILITY AGREEMENTS.—(1) Inspections of
12 plants, plant sites, or other facilities or locations for which
13 the United States has a facility agreement with the Orga-
14 nization for the Prohibition of Chemical Weapons shall be
15 conducted in accordance with the facility agreement.

16 (2) Facility agreements shall be concluded for plants,
17 plant sites, or other facilities or locations that are subject
18 to inspection pursuant to paragraph 4 of Article VI of the
19 Chemical Weapons Convention unless the owner and the
20 operator, occupant or agent in charge of the facility and
21 the Technical Secretariat agree that such an agreement
22 is not necessary. Facility agreements should be concluded
23 for plants, plant sites, or other facilities or locations that
24 are subject to inspection pursuant to paragraphs 5 or 6
25 of Article VI of the Chemical Weapons Convention if so

1 requested by the owner and the operator, occupant or

2 agent in charge of the facility.

3   (3) The owner and the operator, occupant or agent

4 in charge shall, to the extent practicable consistent with

5 the obligations of the United States under the Chemical

6 Weapons Convention, participate in the negotiation of all

7 facility agreements concluded pursuant to the Convention.

8   (g) SAMPLING AND SAFETY.—(1) The Department of

9 Commerce is authorized to require the provision of sam-

10 ples to a member of the inspection team of the Technical

11 Secretariat in accordance with the provisions of the Chem-

12 ical Weapons Convention. The owner or the operator, oc-

13 cupant or agent in charge of the premises to be inspected

14 shall determine whether the sample shall be taken by rep-

15 resentatives of the premises or the inspection team or

16 other individuals present.

17   (2) In carrying out their activities, members of the

18 inspection team of the Technical Secretariat and rep-

19 resentatives of agencies or departments accompanying the

20 inspection team shall observe safety regulations estab-

21 lished at the premises to be inspected, including those for

22 protection of controlled environments within a facility and

23 for personal safety.

24   (h) COORDINATION.—To the extent possible consist-

25 ent with the obligations of the United States pursuant to

1 the Chemical Weapons Convention, the representatives of
2 the United States National Authority, the Department of
3 Commerce and any other agency or department, if
4 present, shall assist the owner and the operator, occupant
5 or agent in charge of the premises to be inspected in inter-
6 acting with the members of the inspection team of the
7 Technical Secretariat.

8 **SEC. 402. OTHER INSPECTIONS AND LEAD AGENCY.**

9   (a) OTHER INSPECTIONS.—The provisions of this
10 title shall apply, as appropriate, to all other inspections
11 authorized by the Chemical Weapons Convention. For all
12 inspections other than those conducted pursuant to para-
13 graphs 4, 5, or 6 of Article VI of the Convention, the term
14 "Department of Commerce" shall be replaced by the term
15 "Lead Agency" in section 401.

16   (b) LEAD AGENCY.—For the purposes of this title,
17 the term "Lead Agency" means the agency or department
18 designated by the President or the designee of the Presi-
19 dent to exercise the functions and powers set forth in the
20 specific provision, based, inter alia, on the particular re-
21 sponsibilities of the agency or department within the
22 United States Government and the relationship of the
23 agency or department to the premises to be inspected.

SEC. 403. PROHIBITED ACTS.

It shall be unlawful for any person to fail or refuse to permit entry or inspection, or to disrupt, delay or otherwise impede an inspection as required by this Act or the Chemical Weapons Convention.

SEC. 404. PENALTIES.

(a) CIVIL.—(1) Any person who violates a provision of section 203, 303, or 403 of this Act shall be liable to the United States for a civil penalty in an amount not to exceed $50,000 for each such violation. For purposes of this subsection, each day such a violation of section 403 continues shall constitute a separate violation of section 403.

(2)(A) A civil penalty for a violation of section 203, 303, or 403 of this Act shall be assessed by the Lead Agency by an order made on the record after opportunity (provided in accordance with this subparagraph) for a hearing in accordance with section 554 of title 5, United States Code. Before issuing such an order, the Lead Agency shall give written notice to the person to be assessed a civil penalty under such order of the Lead Agency's proposal to issue such order and provide such person an opportunity to request, within fifteen days of the date the notice is received by such person, such a hearing on the order.

(B) In determining the amount of a civil penalty, the
2 Lead Agency shall take into account the nature, cir-
3 cumstances, extent and gravity of the violation or viola-
4 tions and, with respect to the violator, ability to pay, effect
5 on ability to continue to do business, any history of prior
6 such violations, the degree of culpability, and such other
7 matters as justice may require.

8   (C) The Lead Agency may compromise, modify or
9 remit, with or without conditions, any civil penalty which
10 may be imposed under this subsection. The amount of
11 such penalty, when finally determined, or the amount
12 agreed upon in compromise, may be deducted from any
13 sums owing by the United States to the person charged.

14   (3) Any person who requested in accordance with
15 paragraph (2)(A) a hearing respecting the assessment of
16 a civil penalty and who is aggrieved by an order assessing
17 a civil penalty may file a petition for judicial review of
18 such order with the United States Court of Appeals for
19 the District of Columbia Circuit or for any other circuit
20 in which such person resides or transacts business. Such
21 a petition may be filed only within the thirty-day period
22 beginning on the date the order making such assessment
23 was issued.

24   (4) If any person fails to pay an assessment of a civil
25 penalty—

  (A) after the order making the assessment has

2 become a final order and if such person does not file

3 a petition for judicial review of the order in accord-

4 ance with paragraph (3); or

5 (B) after a court in an action brought under

6 paragraph (3) has entered a final judgment in favor

7 of the Lead Agency;

8 the Attorney General shall recover the amount assessed

9 (plus interest at currently prevailing rates from the date

10 of the expiration of the thirty-day period referred to in

11 paragraph (3) or the date of such final judgment, as the

12 case may be) in an action brought in any appropriate dis-

13 trict court of the United States. In such an action, the

14 validity, amount and appropriateness of such penalty shall

15 not be subject to review.

16 (b) CRIMINAL.—Any person who knowingly violates

17 any provision of section 203, 303, or 403 of this Act, shall,

18 in addition to or in lieu of any civil penalty which may

19 be imposed under subsection (a) for such violation, be

20 fined under title 18, United States Code, imprisoned for

21 not more than two years, or both.

22 **SEC. 405. SPECIFIC ENFORCEMENT.**

23 (a) JURISDICTION.—The district courts of the United

24 States shall have jurisdiction over civil action to—

1   (1) restrain any violation of section 203, 303,

2 or 403 of this Act; and

3   (2) compel the taking of any action required by

4 or under this Act or the Chemical Weapons Conven-

5 tion.

6   (b) CIVIL ACTION.—A civil action described in sub-

7 section (a) may be brought—

8   (1) in the case of a civil action described in sub-

9 section (a)(1), in the United States district court for

10 the judicial district wherein any act, omission, or

11 transaction constituting a violation of section 203,

12 303, or 403 of this Act occurred or wherein the de-

13 fendant is found or transacts business; or

14   (2) in the case of a civil action described in sub-

15 section (a)(2), in the United States district court for

16 the judicial district wherein the defendant is found

17 or transacts business.

18 In any such civil action process may be served on a defend-

19 ant wherever the defendant may reside or may be found,

20 whether the defendant resides or may be found within the

21 United States or elsewhere.

22 **SEC. 406. LEGAL PROCEEDINGS.**

23   (a) WARRANTS.—(1) The Lead Agency shall seek the

24 consent of the owner or the operator, occupant or agent

25 in charge of the premises to be inspected prior to the initi-

1 ation of any inspection. Before or after seeking such con-
2 sent, the Lead Agency may seek a search warrant from
3 any official authorized to issue search warrants. Proceed-
4 ings regarding the issuance of a search warrant shall be
5 conducted ex parte, unless otherwise requested by the
6 Lead Agency. The Lead Agency shall provide to the offi-
7 cial authorized to issue search warrants all appropriate in-
8 formation supplied by the Technical Secretariat to the
9 United States National Authority regarding the basis for
10 the selection of the plant site, plant, or other facility or
11 location for the type of inspection sought, including, for
12 challenge inspections pursuant to Article IX of the Chemi-
13 cal Weapons Convention, appropriate evidence or reasons
14 provided by the requesting State Party to the Convention
15 with regard to its concerns about compliance with the
16 Chemical Weapons Convention at the facility or location.
17 The Lead Agency shall also provide any other appropriate
18 information available to it relating to the reasonableness
19 of the selection of the plant, plant site, or other facility
20 or location for the inspection.

21   (2) The official authorized to issue search warrants
22 shall promptly issue a warrant authorizing the requested
23 inspection upon an affidavit submitted by the Lead Agen-
24 cy showing that—

1   (A) the Chemical Weapons Convention is in
2   force for the United States;

3   (B) the plant site, plant, or other facility or lo-
4   cation sought to be inspected is subject to the spe-
5   cific type of inspection requested under the Chemical
6   Weapons Convention;

7   (C) the procedures established under the Chem-
8   ical Weapons Convention and this Act for initiating
9   an inspection have been complied with; and

10   (D) the Lead Agency will ensure that the in-
11   spection is conducted in a reasonable manner and
12   will not exceed the scope or duration set forth in or
13   authorized by the Chemical Weapons Convention or
14   this Act.

15   (3) The warrant shall specify the type of inspection
16 authorized; the purpose of the inspection; the type of plant
17 site, plant, or other facility or location to be inspected;
18 to the extent possible, the items, documents and areas that
19 may be inspected; the earliest commencement and latest
20 concluding dates and times of the inspection; and the iden-
21 tities of the representatives of the Technical Secretariat,
22 if known, and, if applicable, the representatives of agencies
23 or departments.

24   (b) SUBPOENAS.—In carrying out this Act, the Lead
25 Agency may by subpoena require the attendance and testi-

mony of witnesses and the production of reports, papers, documents, answers to questions and other information that the Lead Agency deems necessary. Witnesses shall be paid the same fees and mileage that are paid witnesses in the courts of the United States. In the event of contumacy, failure or refusal of any person to obey any such subpoena, any district court of the United States in which venue is proper shall have jurisdiction to order any such person to comply with such subpoena. Any failure to obey such an order of the court is punishable by the court as a contempt thereof.

(c) INJUNCTIONS AND OTHER ORDERS.—No court shall issue an injunction or other order that would limit the ability of the Technical Secretariat to conduct, or the United States National Authority or the Lead Agency to facilitate, inspections as required or authorized by the Chemical Weapons Convention.

SEC. 407. AUTHORITY.

The Lead Agency may issue such regulations as are necessary to implement this title and the provisions of the Chemical Weapons Convention, and amend or revise them as necessary. The Lead Agency shall have the authority to appoint officials to issue warrants pursuant to section 406(a) authorizing inspections pursuant to this title.

APPENDIX 2

UNITED STATES ARMS CONTROL AND DISARMAMENT AGENCY
Washington, D C 20451

November 29, 1994

Dear Mr. Chairman:

You have asked for a legal opinion concerning the adequacy of the Fourth Amendment protections contained in the provisions of the proposed Chemical Weapons Convention Implementation Act of 1994 (the Act). The Administration believes that the provisions of the Chemical Weapons Convention (CWC) and the Act fully protect citizens of the United States, including corporations, from unreasonable searches and seizures.

As an initial matter, the Administration anticipates that access to private facilities will be voluntarily granted for the vast majority of inspections under the CWC. The Supreme Court has held that where valid consent to search is obtained, the protections under the Fourth Amendment are waived, including the need to obtain a search warrant. Therefore, the Administration believes that Fourth Amendment concerns might conceivably arise in only a small number of instances in which access is not voluntarily granted.

In these presumably rare cases the Administration believes that obtaining a search warrant will be the most effective means of ensuring that a search pursuant to the CWC does not violate the inspected person's Fourth Amendment rights. Accordingly, for either a "routine" or "challenge" inspection the Act contains procedures for requesting and issuing a search warrant from any official authorized to issue search warrants in accordance with the Fourth Amendment. The Government anticipates that either administrative search warrants or criminal search warrants will be sought in these situations, depending on the type of inspection and the circumstances surrounding the inspection request.

The Honorable
Lee H. Hamilton
Chairman
Committee on Foreign Affairs
U S. House of Representatives

Routine Inspections

Routine inspections, by their very nature, are not conducted pursuant to a suspicion of a treaty violation, and therefore could not meet the "probable cause" standard required for the issuance of a criminal search warrant. As a result, in the event that access is not provided on a voluntary basis for a routine inspection of a private facility, the Government will seek to obtain an administrative search warrant. Such a warrant is issued on the basis of "administrative probable cause," i.e., inter alia, a finding that there exists a reasonable administrative scheme for conducting inspections authorized by, and in furtherance of, explicit legislation, and that the object of the inspection fits within that scheme and was chosen by neutral and objective criteria.

When requesting an administrative search warrant under the Act, the Government must provide to the official authorized to issue search warrants all appropriate information supplied by the Technical Secretariat of the CWC's Organization for the Prohibition of Chemical Weapons (OPCW) regarding the basis for the selection of the facility or location. The Government would also be required to provide any other appropriate information available to it relating to the reasonableness of the selection of the location for the inspection.

Challenge Inspections

Challenge inspections are conducted upon the request of a State Party to the CWC that has a specific concern about compliance with the Convention. In addition to the criteria discussed above, there is judicial authority for granting administrative search warrants for suspected specific violations, which are granted pursuant to a standard of probable cause different from that applied to criminal search warrants. Accordingly, the Administration believes that administrative search warrants can be used for the majority of non-consensual challenge inspections. If the evidence provided by the Technical Secretariat meets criminal probable cause standards, however, the Act leaves open the possibility of obtaining a criminal search warrant.

When requesting a warrant for a challenge inspection, the Government must provide to the official authorized to issue search warrants the same information as is required for a routine inspection. In addition, for challenge inspections, the Government must submit appropriate evidence or reasons provided by the requesting State Party with regard to its concerns about compliance with the Convention at the facility or location.

It should be noted that, at U.S. insistence, the CWC explicitly allows an inspected Party to "tak[e] into account... [its] constitutional obligations...with regard to... searches and seizures" when providing access for a challenge inspection. Therefore, the United States would not be in violation of the Convention if this process resulted in the Government being required to limit access by the inspection team on the basis of the Fourth

Amendment's prohibition of unreasonable searches and seizures.

Issuance of Warrants

Once the appropriate information is provided, the Act directs the authorized official to issue promptly a search warrant authorizing the requested routine or challenge inspection if: an affidavit is submitted by the Government showing that the CWC is in force for the United States; the facility to be inspected is subject to the specific type of inspection requested; the procedures established under the CWC and the Act for initiating an inspection have been complied with; and the Government undertakes to ensure that the inspection is conducted in a reasonable manner and will not exceed the scope or duration set forth in or authorized by the CWC or the implementing legislation. The warrant must specify: the type of inspection authorized; the purpose of the inspection; the type of facility to be inspected; the items, documents and areas that may be inspected; the commencement and concluding dates and times of the inspection; and the identities of the representative of the Technical Secretariat of the OPCW, if known, and, if applicable, the representatives of the U.S. Government.

Additional Protections

The inspection regime set forth in the Act is patterned after similar administrative inspection regimes already in force in the United States, e.g., inspections of chemical industry under the Toxic Substances Control Act. Accordingly, regardless of whether the inspection is conducted voluntarily or involuntarily, as with these other schemes the proposed legislation contains a number of provisions designed to protect individual rights.

Under the Act, written notice must be provided to the owner and to the operator, occupant or agent in charge of the premises to be inspected (although failure to receive a notice will not prevent an inspection). The notice must be submitted to the owner/operator as soon as possible after the Government receives it from the Technical Secretariat of the OPCW. The notice must include all appropriate information supplied by the Technical Secretariat regarding the basis for the selection of the facility, including, for challenge inspections, appropriate evidence or reasons provided by the requesting State Party with regard to that State Party's concerns.

In addition, the Act provides that if the owner, operator, occupant or agent in charge of the premises is present, a member of the inspection team and, if present, the U.S. Government representative must present appropriate credentials. Consistent with the timeframes in the CWC, each inspection must be commenced and completed with reasonable promptness and conducted at reasonable times, within reasonable limits, and in a reasonable manner. The Government must endeavor to ensure that, to the extent possible consistent with the CWC, each inspection is commenced, conducted and concluded during ordinary working hours. It must be noted, however, that the timelines under the CWC are in continuous hours; therefore, inspectors have a right to work around-the-clock. To the extent possible consistent with the CWC, no inspection can extend to financial, sales and marketing (other than shipment), pricing, personnel, research, or patent data, or data maintained for compliance with environmental or occupational health and safety regulations.

Finally, under the Act, if the U.S. has signed a facility agreement with the OPCW, any routine inspection of that facility must be conducted in accordance with the facility agreement. Because a facility agreement will establish mandatory detailed inspection procedures for a facility, the Administration believes that the conclusion of a facility agreement will encourage owners, operators, occupants or agents in charge of facilities subject to inspection under the CWC to voluntarily grant access to their facilities. Furthermore, even if access is denied, a facility agreement will provide additional protections for the owner, operator, occupant or agent in charge of the premises of a facility by limiting the scope of inspection activities to those contained in the agreement.

Under the CWC and the Act, facility agreements must be concluded for all Schedule 1 facilities and for Schedule 2 facilities, unless the owner and the operator, occupant or agent in charge of the premises and the Technical Secretariat of the OPCW agree that such an agreement is not necessary. The owners and the operators, occupants or agents in charge of the premises of Schedule 3 facilities, and other chemical production facilities subject to inspections pursuant to Part IX of the Verification Annex of the CWC, have the option to request a facility agreement. The Act provides that, if a request is made, the United States Government should conclude a facility agreement for that facility. It should be noted that, under the Act, the owner and the operator, occupant or agent in charge of the premises shall have the right, to the extent practicable consistent with the obligations of the U.S. under the CWC, to participate in the negotiation of all facility agreements.

The Administration believes that these procedures fully protect individual rights under the Fourth Amendment.

The Office of Management and Budget advises that there is no objection to the submission of this report to Congress from the standpoint of the Administration's program.

Sincerely,

Ivo Spalatin
Director of Congressional Affairs

O

CPSIA information can be obtained
at www.ICGtesting.com
Printed in the USA
BVHW040914211218
536170BV00015B/435/P